ST. ANDREW'S BEBINGTON

A HISTORY
OF
ST ANDREW'S PARISH CHURCH

by

Richard Lancelyn Green

First published 1993 by Countyvise Limited, 1 & 3 Grove Road, Rock Ferry, Birkenhead, Wirral, Merseyside L42 3XS

Photoset and printed by Birkenhead Press Limited, 1 & 3 Grove Road, Rock Ferry, Birkenhead, Wirral, Merseyside L42 3AX

ISBN 0 907768 58 X

FOREWORD

For the people of Bebington their parish church is a place of history and hope. It is no accident that a St. Andrew's flag appears in the centre of the town's coat of arms, because the church of that name has served the community since Saxon times.

This book is published in connection with St. Andrew's 900th Anniversary celebrations and Richard Lancelyn Green is to be congratulated as the author of a valuable new history. His own family is caught up in the story and the year 1093 records his forebears witnessing the passage of St. Andrew's into the care of the Benedictine monks, then newly arrived in Chester. More recently the author's father, Roger Lancelyn Green, wrote about the church and we are grateful to Richard for his fresh research and the style he has brought to this new work.

It is good to read of the past and to trace the town's history in the development of the building and the spread of daughter churches. Through many changes, St. Andrew's spire has pointed the eyes of people upwards to find their hope in God. Despite wars and hardship, He has proved faithful to those who have trusted Him in every generation. The message of the early Bible-loving monks from Cluny spoke of peace and life for those who would follow Jesus Christ as Lord. Some things do not change and that same good news excites both speaker and listener on the same site today.

I am glad that this book has been written and pray that the preaching and caring ministry of Christians at St. Andrew's will continue to hold a central place in Bebington's future as it has done in her past.

GEOFF TURNER

CONTENTS

A HISTORY OF ST ANDREW'S PARISH CHURCH

THE SAXON CHURCH

According to tradition Christianity was brought to Bebington by St Patrick in AD 432 and after a lapse back to paganism was re-introduced by St Chad in about 670. The earliest church at Bebington is thought to have been built of wood or wattle and daub and probably preceded King Athelstan's defeat of the Danish and Irish forces at the Battle of Brunenburgh in 937 which made the area safe from further invasion. It was replaced shortly before the Norman Conquest by a stone building known as the 'Whitchurch' or 'White Church'. Ormerod, the Cheshire historian, following an authority on Bede says this was the name 'commonly given to the new or Saxon buildings of stone, which had taken the place of the former wooden ones', but others believe it was so named because of the distinctive cream-white stone hewn from the Roman quarries at Storeton. A weathered line of stone below the south nave wall is of a different class of masonry from the Norman structure above and shows that the Saxon church was contained within the present south aisle. The nave was thirty feet in length, while the chancel was fifteen feet. The chancel was on a lower level and was slightly deflected to the north.

A curious legend connected with the building of the church is mentioned by Philip Sulley in *The Hundred of Wirral* (1889). It is said 'that it was intended to build on a site nearer Tranmere, and the stone was carted there in the daytime, but carried to its present site during the night, and that this occurred so repeatedly that finally it became necessary to build it there'.

In Saxon times the Wirral peninsula was richly forested and the settlements or 'tunes' (from which the 'ton' endings are derived) consisted of a wall or stockade surrounding small houses and barns. Bebington still maintains a link with its distant past in the names of the roads around the church, such as The Wiend and Kirket Lane. The village itself is said to have been named after a Saxon chieftain or landowner called 'Bebba' and has always had close links with Poulton (the 'tune by the pool') where there was a castle or fortified dwelling overlooking the 'Marfords' (Mere Ford) on the road to Bromborough. The *Domesday Book* reveals that in the days of Edward the Confessor, Poulton and the church at Bebington were held by a freeman called Gamel (possibly Gamel Fitz Grifin, a privileged thane). The manor was abandoned at the time of the Conquest and passed with the rest of Wirral into the hands of

Hugh Lupus, the first Earl of Chester. He divided the settlements among his barons, granting Poulton and Bebington ('Pontone') to Osbern Fitz Tezzon (of Dodleston). Fitz Tezzon in turn left the management to 'Roger' who may have been a Saxon relative of the original owner.

The *Domesday Book* lists 'Pontone' as one of several places held by Osbern Fitz Tezzon:

> The same Osbern holds Pontone and Roger [holds it of him]. Gamel held it and was a free man. There [are] 2 hides that pay gold. The land is for 4 ploughs. In demesne is 1 [plough] and 2 serfs, and 1 radman and 1 villein and a priest and 4 bordars with 1 plough between them all. During the reign of Edward it was worth 25s and afterwards it was waste. Now it is worth 25s.

THE EARLIEST RECORDS

The first specific reference to Bebington and the church comes in 1093 when Scirard (or 'Seward') gave the 'chapel' and several acres of land to the Abbey of St Werburgh in Chester. He was the first of the de Lancelyns (or 'Launcelins') and his Saxon sounding Christian name was an anglicised form of 'Gerard'. His forebears came from Beaugency in Normandy and he was one of the settlers brought over by the barons in 1070 to replace the Saxon owners. He was the first Lord of the Manor of Poulton and Bebington (whose descendants still retain the title) and he held the manor in fee to Hugo Fitz Tezzon. His possession was confirmed by a charter of Hugh de Boidele, the great-grandson of Osbern Fitz Tezzon and was in exchange for twenty marks and the services of four men to assist every third year in the repairs of the castle and earthworks of Dodleston (later commuted to two silver pence per year, and the attendance of two men at Dodleston Castle for three days every third year).

The church was given as an endowment for the new Benedictine Abbey of St Werburgh in Chester which had been founded the previous year by Earl Hugh on the site of a church of secular Canons. The Charter of Confirmation or Foundation Charter of the Abbey states that in 1093: 'Seward dedit capellam de Bebinton, et terram quartuor boum, et deciman illius manerii'. The gift was witnessed by Hugo Fitz Tezzon, the superior lord, and was confirmed by Earl Hugh and his wife, the Countess Ermentrude. The gift included a tenth of five manors, and a third part of Scirard's substance to be given after the death of himself and his wife.

Several later charters confirmed the gift of the advowson by the Lancelyns. One was addressed to Earl Ranulf II in 1150; another was to

Richard, Archbishop of Canterbury in 1170 (by Robert Lancelyn); and there were a series of charters and concords in 1272 between William Lancelyn and the Abbot Simon.

THE NORMAN CHURCH

The church was rebuilt in 1120-30. The south and west walls and the porch of the old building were incorporated into a new church four times the original size. The nave was in the present south or Poulton Aisle and the chancel was on the site of the Feilden Chapel. A narrow north aisle ran the length of the church. It was divided from the nave by five free standing pillars and from the Chancel by a single pillar. Two of the pillars survive in their original form. They are two feet in diameter, eleven feet high, and are topped with reeded caps and square abaci. A third, which stood at the west end, was later partly incorporated into the wall. A fourth was removed and the arch widened early in the nineteenth century and the fifth which had been moved in and formed an unsightly join between the Norman and Tudor sections was removed in 1847. The arches above the surviving pillars and the lower section of the south wall are survivals of the early Norman building, as is the upper part of the font.

The nave of the Norman church was forty feet in length and extended as far as the conical corbel on the south wall, but the appearance of the eastern end can only be surmised from parts discovered in the wall. The foundations show that the chancel and the narrow northern part were on a lower level (as in the earlier church) and had a slight deflection. The remains of two half pillars, seven capitals, and an equal number of bases are embedded in the west wall (with the carved and moulded portions turned inward and partly squared off, and disguised by fake mortar joints). A large capital and part of a base were also retrieved from the western gable in 1897, and there is a corbel near the roof on the left of the west window made from Norman fragments. These suggest that the east end had one free standing pillar dividing the chancel from the narrow north aisle, while the half pillars supported the arches between the two sections.

The quality of the Norman architecture implies that the church was of importance, and it grew more powerful with the founding of a Chapel at Poulton-cum-Spital. This was dedicated to Thomas A'Becket or 'Thomas the Martyr' and served as a hospital for lepers. It was established soon after Becket's death and was confirmed by his immediate successor (who died in 1183). The charter is in the name of Richard, Archbishop of Canterbury, and lists various endowments including a carucate of land, half a fishery, and part of a wood. It makes clear that these do not encroach upon the endowments or rights of the 'mother church' at Bebington ('salvo jure matris ecclesiae de Bebinton'). Divine service was performd there by the Almoner of the Abbey of St Werburgh (who received the revenues of the Parish of Ince) and Masses were said for the souls of the Bishops of Coventry, and for the Earls, Abbots, and monks of Chester. The chapel is mentioned in the will of William de Lancelyn in 1332, but no later records are known and no trace of the buildings have been found. The name survives at 'Spital crossroads', and Spital Hall was marked on the first Ordinance Survey maps as the site of the chapel.

THE THIRTEENTH CENTURY EXTENSION

Between 1274 and 1280 William de Launcelyn confirmed the original gift of the church at Bebington to St Werburgh's through his father, grandfather and great-grandfather and this may indicate a change of status from parish to collegiate church. It is possible that the services which had been held at the Chapel of St Thomas were transferred to Bebington after plague had decimated the community. The records show a growth in the prosperity of the church at that time, and throughout the second half of the thirteenth century it paid a yearly pension of 2 marks to the abbey in Chester. Collegiate status required a body of permanent clergy or 'colleagues' under the Rector who performed the full round of services by day and night. The stalls with misericords would be consistent with this (the 'misericord' being an indulgence for those who had to stand during the long services).

The last vestiges of the Saxon church were removed in about 1280. The south wall and the Spital porch were rebuilt in the Early Decorated style, and the windows on either side were enlarged. The sill heights remained at different levels (reflecting the floor levels of the original Saxon building). The south porch remains almost unaltered. It has an outer door of two thicknesses of inch oak fixed perpendicularly, and there are stone seats on either side. These were used by the elderly when the church was unpewed and when parts of the services were held at the church door. The inner doorway has a drop arch and is surmounted by a hood mould on bosses.

The thirteenth century ashlar masonry on the inside of the south wall 'batters' or slopes outwards at the top and was intended to take plaster. It was covered with floral frescoes. Fragments round the South Porch and others on the west wall were revealed in 1897 when the later plaster and whitewash was removed.

THE FOURTEENTH CENTURY NORTH AISLE AND CHANCEL

Further alterations were made in 1320, but they have been superseded by later work. The narrow north aisle was widened and converted into the nave, and a new chancel was built. The windows and porch in the north wall date from this period but only parts are original as they were dismantled and rebuilt in their present position in 1847 when the north aisle was extended. There is no trace of the Second Pointed Chancel, other than a fragment supposed to have come from the main window.

THE TUDOR CHURCH

The east end of the church was entirely rebuilt in the Tudor period and a tradition has grown that the last Abbot of St Werburgh, Dr John Clarke decided to make use of surplus funds from the Abbey's treasury to prevent its sequestration by the King. The work is said to have been given added urgency following the closure of the smaller monasteries in 1535 and to have been brought to an abrupt end after the dissolution of the Abbey in 1540. This theory was put forward by the late nineteenth century antiquaries and sounds very convincing, but an earlier date must be preferred as the Church is known to have possessed a stained glass window dated '1523'. The Masons' marks also show that the Tudor building was started in about 1520 and finished no later than 1530. Thus it may be that the families whose coats of arms were represented on the windows, the Lancelyns, the Mynshulls, and the Stanleys and Chauntrells were the benefactors of the church, and perhaps competed with each other to build the three aisles. The earlier date brings the rebuilding within the Rectorship of John Brereton (1511-28) who was the Master Mason for Cheshire and Flint, and known for other churches which he built, such as that at Astbury. It seems that he was responsible, while the cost was met by the landowners, perhaps with some assistance from the Abbey. It is also possible that the plans were instigated by Brereton's predecessor Nicholas Chauntrell (1507-11). He was a member of a family who owned land in Bebington and his parents were commemorated in the the window of 1523. The work presumably came to an end in 1528 when John Brereton left Bebington.

The Tudor section consists of the three bays of the chancel and north and south aisles and the first bay of the nave. It is on a slightly different alignment from the Norman part which suggests that the whole church was to have been rebuilt. The chancel extends only a few feet further than the side aisles-as in other Cheshire churches, but is unique in having a high clerestory window on the south return. The main east window is unusual as it incorporates features of two styles. The upright principal and secondary mullions are Perpendicular, while the curvatures of the central mullions are in the Decorated style. It has five lights and there is no cusping in the upper part. Under the window on the exterior there are stone corbels to support the roof of a vestry or robing room (to which there was access by a small door at the right of the altar) and also a recess or aumbry. If the corbels were used at the time there was presumably a stone-built, battlemented structure, but it is more likely that the vestry was added later.

The two side aisles are similar in style, but not identical. The large number of Masons' marks show that the work was carried out by many hands and the cusping on the windows and the carved surrounds differ in almost every particular. Both aisles were designed with chapels and they had brackets for lamps. Those in the north have been removed, but they survive in the south where there is also a Piscina (which was used for washing Holy vessels).

There are four large windows on the north and south sides with slender pillars rising between them and stone panelling below. The main piers are massive clustered shafts of lozenge shape set with the longer axis running north and south. The fluting rises to a delicate collar or half capital and carries through ogee arches. There are columns between them matching those on the side walls and rising to corbels for the roof beams. There is also a blind storey above which raises the height of the Tudor section ten feet above the Norman nave. The whole effect is superb and it is a very confident expression of the architecture of the period.

Ormerod and others believed that the corbels were intended to carry a vaulted stone ceiling rather than one of wood, but this is unlikely as the width of the roof would have required thicker walls or flying buttresses. It was also his belief that the architects of the newer section intended a transept crossing with four large pillars surmounted by a tower, but this too is unlikely. The tower and spire were built only a short time before, and the present appearance of the four pillars is deceptive as two were only enlarged during the Victorian period. There were two large pillars forming the transition from chancel to nave, while the other two were half pillars of no great strength. There was also no arch or wall across the nave. This was added during a later restoration when the rough edges were tidied up and the pillars strengthened.

The rebuilding came to a sudden end leaving a gap between the two halves. The outer walls were joined and a Norman pillar which had been displaced was resited near the new pillar. This made the difference in the alignment between the old and new nave all the more obvious as the small lath and plaster arch and walling in the arcade was at a pronounced angle. The old section of the central aisle was slightly wider than the new, and the north aisle ended in a rough plain wall.

The old stained glass (which is now lost) was contemporary with the building. Fortunately it was described by Thomas Chaloner or by one of the Randle Holmes in some manuscript notes dated 1629 (Harleian MS 2151). There were three windows which contained the armorial bearings of local landowners. 'In the high window on ye pulpit [side]' were the arms of the Lancelyn family (the Lords of the Manor of Poulton and Lower Bebington). 'In the highest windows on the South side' were those of the Stanleys of Hooton and the Chauntrells; and 'the third window on the north side' had the arms of Mynshull and Bebington. Under the Chauntrell window were the words: 'Orate p. bono statu Rici Chauntrell et Margarett ux. eis qui hanc fenestram fieri fect ano. dni. m ccc xxiij ('Pray for the good estate of Richard Chauntrell and Margaret his wife who caused this window to be made, AD 1523'), and under that of the Mynshull's: 'Orate pro bono statu Edwi Mynssuls et Elizabeth ux. eius ('Pray for the good estate of Edward Mynshull and Elizabeth his wife'. The manuscript (which abbreviates the inscriptions) identifies Richard and Margaret Chauntrell as the parents of Nicholas Chauntrell, Rector of Bebington (1507-11). Edward Mynshull was the son of John Mynshull (1448-1527), and a descendant of the Bebingtons who were the first Lords of the Manor of Higher Bebington. The manuscript gives drawings of the four shields. [1] Lancelyn: Argent, on a fesse Sable three mullets of the first pierced of the second; [2] Stanley Hooton: Quarterly first and fourth for Stanley - Argent on a band Azure three stags' heads, cabossed Or; second and third for Hooton - blank [but should have been Argent on a bend Azure, three Mullets Or]; [3] Chauntrell, blank [but should be Azure, a pelican in her nest feeding young, Argent]; [4] 'Minssull Bebington': Quarterly first and fourth for Mynshull - Azure, three estoiles Argent in the fesse plus point a crescent [of the last]; second and third for Bebington - Sable, three stags' heads cabossed, Argent.

Most of this glass was destroyed during the Commonwealth period, but the Rev. T.B. Banner, who was curate at Bebington before the 1847 restoration, remembered 'some excellent painted glass' in the south aisle. And even after the restoration pieces of early glass remained. 'A few bits exist,' said Charles Reed in 1848, 'as old thread remains, though the garment has been through the fire, irregularly put together in some of the windows; with the various colours, but without the regularity, of the kaleidoscope.'

The church had stone flags and it is unlikely that there were ever any tiles either on the floor or walls, but one tile from the late fifteenth or early sixteenth century was discovered last century in a garden at Mersey Terrace, Bebington, and was claimed at the time to have come from the church. 'It is interesting,' said the inscription in the Mayer Museum, 'as probably having belonged to the Old Church not far distant from where it was found as well as from the quaint inscription upon it which is drawn in a white slip or glaze upon brown glaze ground which *in modern english* reads thus:

Remember thy life
May not ever endure
That thou doest thyself
Of that thou art sure
But that thou keepest
Unto thy future cure
And ever it availe thee
It is but adventure [chance]'

The Church from the East

THE SEVENTEENTH CENTURY

Very few changes were made to the church during the seventeenth century. The lamps which had burnt on the brackets had already been extinguished when the Chantries were closed during the reign of Edward VI, and during the Commonwealth period the building was denuded of much of its furniture and fittings. This included the Rood screen which divided the chancel from the nave. Evidence of it came to light during the restoration of 1846 when the grooves were revealed in the pillars, and part of the wooden cross was discovered in the graveyard where it had been buried in 1643. The Jacobean Bishop's throne and the carved stalls survived, and tradition has it that the altar table and the rails were discarded in 1640 and taken to Poulton Hall (where a table and bannisters of the appropriate date may still be seen).

William Smith and William Webb in their gazetteer of the 'Vale-Royall' (1656) described Nether Bebington as 'a church-town, with a fair Church, and goodly parsonage', while at Over Bebington 'John Minshal of Minshal Esquire, hath great store of good Possessions'. Peter Leycester in his *Historical Antiquities of Great Britain and Ireland* (1673) mentions only that the Stanleys of Hooton acted as Patrons of Bebington Parish Church (and that they were in dispute with the Dean of Chester over patronage of Eastham church).

THE EIGHTEENTH CENTURY

A clearer picture is possible after 1774 when the Parish Accounts begin and there is a painting of the church dating from about 1790. A visitor at that time would have been greeted by rows of box pews, while in the chancel there was the high pulpit with staircase, a clerk's desk, and reading desk, and much of the old carved woodwork, including six stalls with misericords set in a single row. The font was at the west end of the central aisle in the darkest part of the church, but several plain windows had been added in the wall between the Norman and Tudor sections. Attempts had also been made to modernise the church by coating all the walls with whitewash and by covering the beams with lath and plaster ceilings. Recent additions had included the memorials to the Greens of Poulton Lancelyn (who were enjoying a period of quiet prosperity while the other great landowners were in decline).

Bebington was a quiet village, though until the turnpike road was built coaches passed through it on the way to Chester. The view across the fields to the Mersey and beyond to Liverpool was uninterrupted and no one then suspected that the population would expand ten fold as a result of the Industrial Revolution.

The first accounts include the purchase of the book itself. On 15 April 1775: 'Bought a book for the Parish to Enter the Church Wardens' Accts. in. £1-2-0', and above there are some earlier expenses, including the celebration on the 5th November when the bells were rung. The cost of entertaining the ringers was 3/6d, and 1/3d was spent on 'Oyl and Candles'.

Some expenses now seem unusual, such as the purchase of sparrows and foxes (a way of keeping them down). It continued until 1794 when it was 'ordered that the Church Wardens do not pay for any more Sparrows or Foxes, until each order be again made for such payments'. Another dramatic incident occurs in 1829: 'Pd. Going to Liverpool when Church was robbed and printing handbills', and later: £5 'Pd. Liverpool Police Officer for apprehending Thos. Jones for Breaking in the Church and Stealing Prayer Book from thence', and 3/- 'By cash for Ferry & expense going to L'pool to Pay the above reward.'

The entries are not always explicit but it is clear that the upkeep of the church was a constant drain on the resources. There were new flagstones in 1777, again in 1821 (when the Tranmere and Storeton aisles were repaved), and other repairs to the floor in 1827, 1828, 1833, and 1834. The interior of the church was whitewashed in 1796, 1810, 1820, and 1828. Seventy-five pews were painted and numbered in 1797 (at a cost of 4d per pew), and green baize was purchased for them in 1776 and 1832. In 1817 a Mr Leigh was paid £14.4.5d for 'Writing the Commandments and Painting the Communion Rails', and they were repainted in 1834. Various foot stools, reading desks, altar coverings, carpets, and other such items were added at different times, but the major outlay was always on the roof and walls.

In 1777 the roofs of the Tranmere and Storeton aisles were stripped of their lead and rebuilt. The lead was sold for £87.6.9d and this partly covered the cost of new timber and the slates. More slates were purchased at regular intervals (three thousand in 1801, a cart load in 1815, and another thousand in 1821), but the beams supporting the roofs were left. The guttering and windows were also replaced, and in 1800 the west wall of the Tranmere aisle was rebuilt.

Some mystery surrounds the vestry at the east end. It is shown in a drawing of 1809 by T.R. Rickman as an undistinguished building with a plain door and window, but no written description survives. It was repaired on several occasions, as was the 'Chancel door' which led to it, and a fire grate was installed in 1810. It may also have been re-roofed in 1822. A quantity of thatch was purchased that year and it is hard to think that it was intended for the main roof -unless it was a temporary covering for some of the oldest and weakest roof timbers. In 1816 Robert McGee was paid £6.9.0d for 'Materials & Plastering & Stucco work done at the Communion', and this may either have been for blocking the chancel door or blocking the clerestory window (which was re-opened in 1847). It is clear that the vestry (which had served as a schoolroom) was disliked by the new Rector, R.M. Feilden, as it was demolished soon after his induction. In May 1827, £1.5.0d was paid 'for taking down the Vestry and Clearing and Carting away the Rubbish'. A new vestry was then constructed at the modest expense of £6.7.7d. This was presumably in the south-east corner as shown on the plans of 1846. It was behind a wooden screen and there was access through the small door in the south wall.

The accounts often fail to specify the nature of the work undertaken and it is not always clear when certain changes were made.

THE EARLY NINETEENTH CENTURY

There is no reference to the small gallery for musicians which was constructed on the south wall. It was approached by stone steps near the South Porch (which started near the buttress) and was entered by a door cut in the wall. Nor is there reference to the door that was cut through the east wall of the North aisle close to the altar and separated from the church by a wooden screen. But details of the large gallery are to be found in the Minutes of the Vestry meeting for 14 October 1829. It was then resolved that in view of the increase in the population which had made the accommodation in the church inadequate 'a gallery be erected at the West or unpewed end of the Church, between the two last Pillars, that is immediately over the pews now occupied by Mr Fitchett and the Church wardens, but not to advance into the Body of the Church beyond those pews, and that the gallery be further extended along some of the sides - the front part of the gallery to contain 16 Pews & capable of containing from 100 to 120 Persons'. The gallery is shown on a plan of the building made in 1846. The screen below ran from the edges of the north and south doorways, and the staircase in the centre had six steps on either side of the second pillar and twenty or so steps leading up and round to the higher level. There were twenty box pews, five on each side of the two aisles and ten in the centre.

A drawing of the church in the late 1830s shows the gallery from the north-east corner. The wooden screen covering the door in the east wall of the north aisle is also visible. Beyond is the Tranmere aisle, half of which was unpewed with a rough stone floor and free standing benches. Against the second pillar there was a modern font on a stone step with kneeling benches around it. The access to the thirteen high boxed pews on either side of the truncated Tranmere aisle is just visible. Turning then to the plan the tour could be continued. One would have passed round the chancel rails to the central aisle where there was a large stove, then down the central aisle past the mediaeval stalls, the pulpit, reading desk and clerk's desk. In the central or Bebington aisle there were eleven box pews on the north side, including the larger ones of the local landowners, and fifteen on the south. The vestry was behind the wooden partition at the south- east corner of the Poulton and Storeton aisle, and there were fifteen pews on the south side of that aisle and nineteen on the north. The numbering of the pews ran from the south-east corner and was in Roman numerals. The pews were let to householders. The 'Pew List' of Richard Green, of Poulton Hall, for 1844, shows that he owned seventeen. The main pew was number 58 directly below the pulpit; his servants used a pew three rows behind, and the others were used by tenant farmers.

Throughout this period the population was continuing to expand at a great rate and the subsequent changes to the church and the creation of several new parishes was a consequence of it. The census returns show the dramatic changes which took place:

	1810	1840	1870
Higher Bebington	191	1,986	3,172
Lower Bebington	279	1,187	3,768
Poulton-Lancelyn	83	155	374
Storeton	179	240	268
Tranmere	474	2,550	16,143

The gallery could not for long statisfy the demand (which was also being met by new churches), and it was also out of tune with the spirit of the age. A change had taken place in church architecture and in people's attitude towards the church buildings. Instead of local builders, joiners, and masons turning their hand to the improvements, large companies who specialised in restoration and the building of new churches were coming into being. Restoration was the order of the day and the Gothic revival was in full swing. Few churches were left unaltered and large sums of money were being spent upon them. The restoration at Woodchurch was one local example and it was the subject of two letters by 'Saxon' (the Rev. William Elstob) in the *Gentleman's Magazine* for 1844. In his first letter he praised the appearance of the restored church, while in the second he contrasted it with the dilapidated condition of the 'once beautiful' church at Bebington:

> I do not say that the church is absolutely in very bad repair, though many of its parts are fast approaching to dilapidation. The whole of the interior should be stripped of its present hideous deformities.

They are chiefly the work of the last century and have been effected at no trifling expense. At least one third of the nave and its aisles have been cut off by a rude screen of timber reaching to the roof, and left in a deplorable condition. A fine old font, which might easily be restored, still remains in this rejected portion of the church, and, like the place wherein it stands, has long ceased to be made use of for its once holy purpose. Within the screen is a western gallery, so wide from back to front as to approach much too nearly to the entrance of the chancel. An organ was erected some years ago, but not in this gallery, for a small one was built to contain it over the little portion that remains of the south aisle. The access to it is of a piece with the rest, and has been gained by breaking a doorway through the south wall. It is approached by a miserable flight of stone steps that would not be thought too good to lead to a hay-loft. Thus disfigured is the otherwise venerable south front. Returning to the interior, we scarcely find a relic of wood-work worthy of being preserved, excepting a few old carved stalls without canopies. They have been ill treated, but are still capable of being brought back to much of their original appearance. Near to these is a very diminutive and unCanonical sort of font, which for many years has been used instead of the real one, and far from 'the accustomed place,' we find it within a few feet of 'the holy table'. I shall conclude by adding that one of the piers on the south side of the nave has been removed and two arches formed into one of the most disproportionate figure and dimensions. Hoping that some good and wealthy Christians will arise and do justice to a church that so intelligibly calls for it.

The call did not go unheeded and by 1846 detailed plans by N.W.L. Moffat for 'enlarging and improving the church' had been made, and on 30 July 1846 an application was made for a Faculty.

THE RESTORATION OF 1846-7

Numerous changes were made. The gallery at the west end and the partition and stairs were removed. The west wall of the Tranmere aisle and the existing north wall were taken down and the aisle was extended to a new west wall containing a window of the same design as that already at the west end. The north wall was rebuilt using the existing stone and window mouldings (with new mullions). The porch was reconstructed in the same style and using many of the original materials. A new arcade corresponding to the Norman one was built with pillars, capitals, bases, and arch mouldings copied from the earlier work. The join between the Norman and Tudor arcade was redesigned with a circular half pillar clamped against the Tudor pier and joined with new footings. The arch

Plan of the church before the restoration of 1847

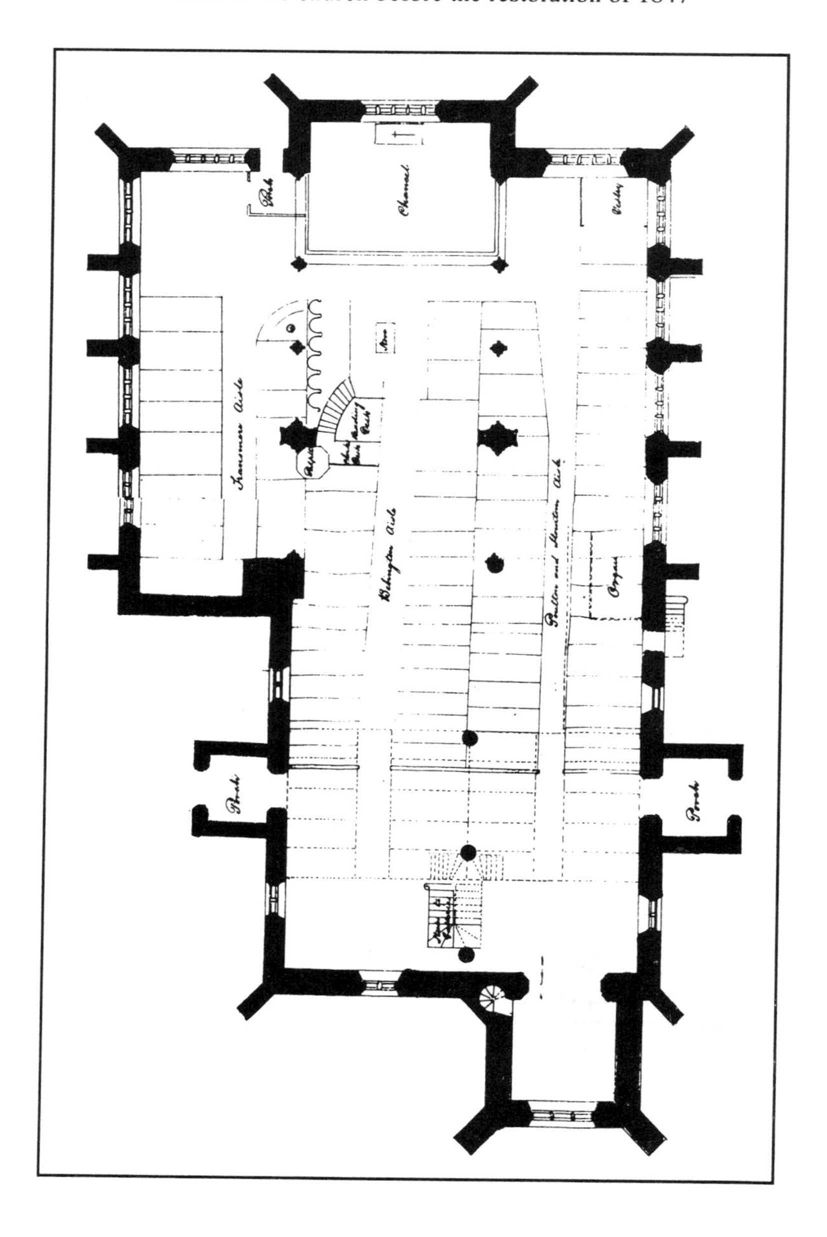

between the Tudor pier and first Norman arch was replaced in lath and plaster, and a corresponding arch on the opposite side was built of stone. A heating chamber was built under the new north aisle (with the flue ingeniously contained in the new pillar above), and ducts were cut under the aisles for the pipes. Repairs were also made to the floor of the ringing chamber in the tower. The lower part was converted into a vestry with a wooden screen dividing it from the church; it was given a Tudor style fireplace and a wall mounted safe. The staircase to the tower from inside the church was blocked and the original exterior door reopened. The organ gallery was removed and the door blocked. The door at the east end of the Tranmere aisle was also blocked and the old flue and chimney taken down. The altar was raised on three steps. The flooring at the west end was renewed and the other flags straightened. The pillars were repaired. The plaster ceilings were removed and the original timbers opened up. The principals were champfered off and the purlins and spars were sanded and stained in dark oak colour. New box pews were made from old timber to match the existing ones. The pulpit and reading desks were altered and the steps were moved to the side of the pillar. The windows were given new leaded lights with wrought iron stay bars and were reglazed with old-style glass in lozenge shaped panes.

THE RESTORED CHURCH

The restoration met with widespread approval. The church was the subject of a paper delivered to the Liverpool Architectural and Archaeological Society by Charles Reed in 1848. He found much to admire and ended by saying, 'there are few country churches of its size in the county of Cheshire so interesting from the various styles of its architecture, so picturesque in its appearance, or so picturesquely situated on a rising mound, whereby its broad and sturdy tower and spire are seen for many miles around.'

Samuel Lewis in his *Topographical Dictionary of England* of 1849 also spoke highly of the church: 'It suffered much by neglect and by injudicious repairs in past years, but has been recently restored, renovated, and considerably enlarged by the liberality of Thomas Green, George Orred Esq. and other spirited contributors, and now presents one of the finest specimens of ecclesiastical architecture in the country.'

The most notable visitor was Nathaniel Hawthorne, the American author who had made his reputation with books such as *The Scarlet Letter*. In 1853 he came to Liverpool as American Consul. He had lodgings in Rock Park and on 8 August 1853, a few days after his arrival, caught sight of the church while on the way to Poulton Hall (which

Plan of the church after the restoration of 1847

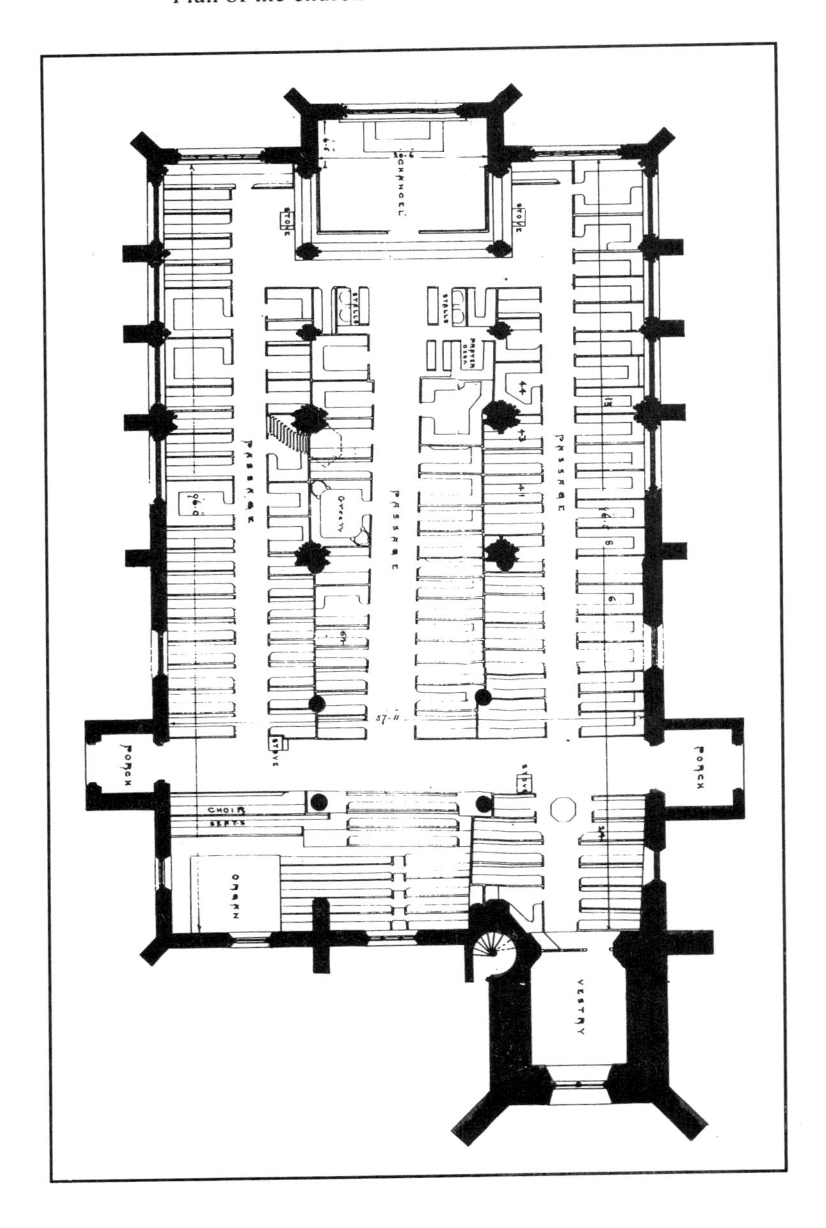

Thomas Green had let to William Barber, the President of the American Chamber of Commerce):

'We passed an old church with a tower and spire, and, half-way up, a patch of ivy, dark-green, and some yellow wall-flowers, in full bloom, growing out of the crevices of the stone. Mr Barber told us that the tower was formerly quite clothed in ivy from bottom to top, but that it had fallen away for lack of the nourishment that it used to find in the lime between the stones. The old church answered to my transatlantic fancies of England better than anything I have yet seen.'

On 29 August 1853 he and his family walked to Bebington and spent some time in the churchyard. The bell was tolling as they came near and many 'respectable looking people' were moving towards it: 'Soon we reached the church, and I have seen nothing yet in England that so completely answered my idea of what such a thing was, as this old village church of Bebington.' They sat for some time examining the graves, looking at the base of the cross, and watching some girls playing in the churchyard. He returned in February 1854 when the bells 'chimed out with a most cheerful sound, and sunny as the morning', and his last visit was in June 1855. He noted then that all the ivy had died away from the spire (as it had been cut at the main root when the door to the tower was re-opened in 1847).

THE RESTORATIONS OF 1871-2 AND 1897

The changes made in 1847 were extensive, but there was still room for improvement. The old pews remained and many were in a decayed condition with rot spreading from the damp earth below. The four new stoves (two on either side of the altar and two at the west end) had also failed to solve the problem of the damp as there was no ventilation. The arrangement of the stalls and desks was also haphazard and outdated by Victorian standards. Four of the six stalls with misericords had survived the earlier restoration and had been made into two pairs facing each other across the central aisle, and the prayer desk had been moved to a position opposite the pulpit. And as ever there was a lack of space.

The solution was to end the obsolete system of letting (which meant pews were left empty when the occupants were abroad) and to provide free pews in their place (as had already been done at the west end when the organ was moved to the north west corner). A committee was established in 1870 to oversee the reseating of the church and W. & G. Audsley of Liverpool were employed as architects. New pews would give an additional two hundred seats, and the rising damp could be cured at the same time. Audsley recommended that the floor be excavated to allow under floor heating and ventilation, that the organ be returned to the centre of the west end, and that the roof be raised with the fake arches replaced in stone. All these things were to be done in time, but at the restoration of 1871-2 the funds were only sufficient to cover the floor and pews.

The work started in July 1871 with Holme and Nichol as the contractors and the church was closed until April 1872. The green baize pews were demolished, and the pulpit, the reading desk, and all the old benches and footstools were discarded (though some of the wood was re-used). For the first time in many centuries it was possible to see the gravestones on the floor, and some of these were relaid after the heating system had been installed. The church was reopened by the Bishop of Chester on 9 April 1872. Every part of the church was then filled with pews of uniform design and all had matching hassocks, and there was a new pulpit and an eagle lectern (given by Harmood Banner) on either side of the chancel arch. The services were also made shorter, and *Hymns: Ancient and Modern* was used for the first time. The roofs, however, were left untouched and these continued to cause problems. By 1895 those over the eastern end could no longer be patched or repaired. Charles E. Deacon was asked to give his advice and he recommended various improvements, including a new roof for the whole church and a stone arch to replace the one in lath and plaster. He also offered to correct the tilt that was apparent in the pier between the Tudor and Norman sections. The work, entrusted to Brown and Backhouse, started in July 1897 and was finished the following January.

The improvements consisted of: a new chancel roof, which replaced the one dating from the fifteenth and seventeenth centuries; new roofs over the side aisles using the old principals and purlins; a new roof over the nave, raised two feet higher than the old one; a stone arch on the south side of the nave to replace the one in lath and plaster; wooden principals in place of the three sham arches aross the eastern end of the nave and aisles which had been put up in wood and plaster in 1847 to conceal the rough principals and the junctions of the Norman and Perdendicular work; the removal of the plaster from the west end of the church, and the cleaning and pointing of all the interior stonework. The cost of over £2000 was defrayed by voluntary contributions. Joseph Balman was Foreman and Clerk of Works; James Corte was Head Joiner, and James Field, Head Mason.

The topping out ceremony was held on 6 December 1897 when a strong glass jar was placed in a cavity over the chancel arch. It contained a parchment scroll listing the improvements, with a silver Diamond Jubilee Medal, a set of Maundy money, four numbers of the Parish

Plan of the church after the restoration of 1872.

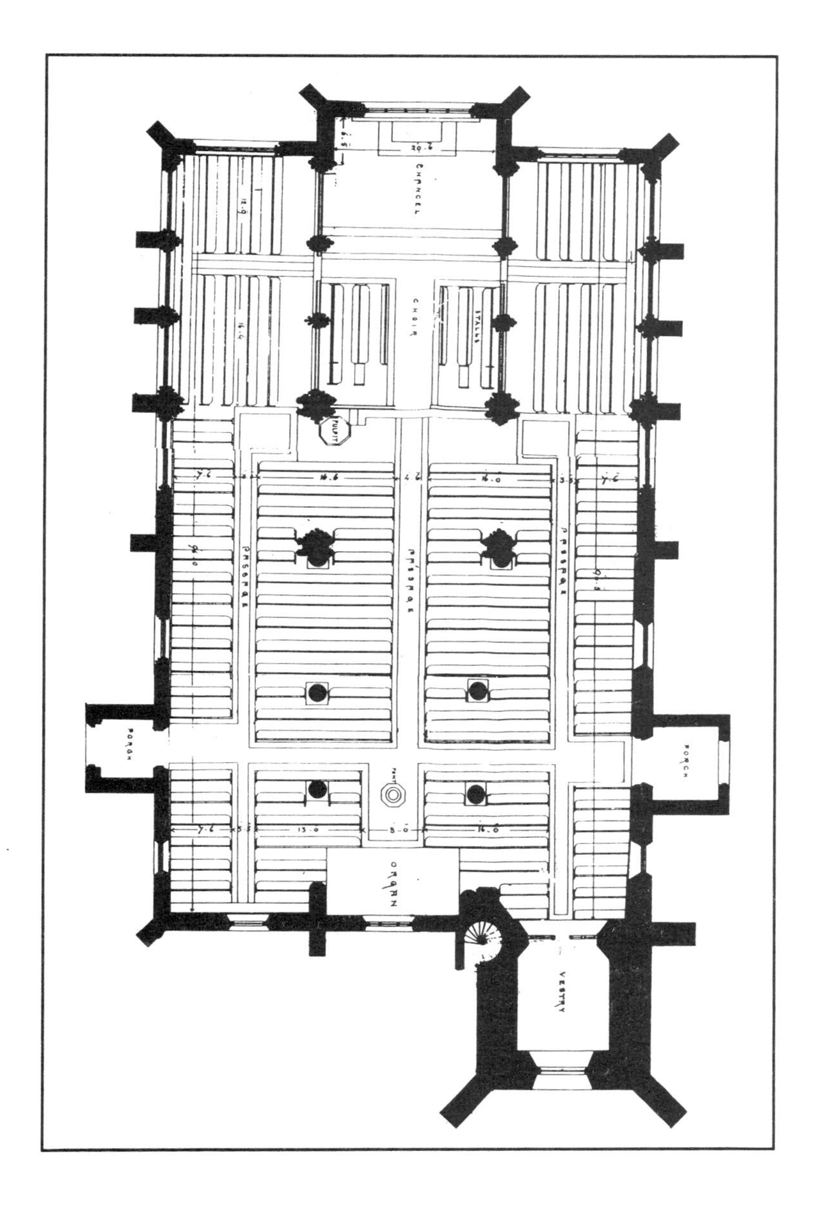

Magazine, a copy of the Chester *Diocesan Gazette*, the Jubilee Numbers of the *Graphic* and *The Times*, and a facsimile of *The Times* of 1838 recording Queen Victoria's Coronation.

A chancel screen designed by Charles E. Deacon and made by Harry Hems of Exeter was given by the Rector and dedicated on 24 September 1898. This did not attempt to copy the original rood screen of which evidence had been found during the restoration. The head of the old screen was nine and a half feet from the nave floor, with a rood-loft above which extended east and west, and had a head coving projecting from the piers. Crosses, given by Andrew Tucker Squarey, were placed on the western gables in January 1899.

The changes and additions made during the present century, such as the construction of the Feilden Memorial Chapel in 1908 are described below with other points of interest. The church was lit by large gas pendants in the Victorian period, and was converted to electricity in 1946.

THE RE-ORDERING OF 1989

In 1989 there was a major internal re-ordering of the Church. The origins go back to the second decade of the century when Mrs. Rainey, the patron, sold the Advowson to the evangelical Church Association, who were the predecessors of the present patrons, The Church Society Trust. In doing so the incumbent - and consequently the Parish - changed from 'High' to 'Low' church, and the new Rectors, from H. E. Boultbee onwards, were anxious to remove the Chancel Screen which Canon Feilden erected in 1898 - as this recalled the High Church theology of the Oxford Movement and was out of tune with the evangelicalism which had replaced it.

A resolution to move the screen was passed at a meeting of the Parochial Church Council in 1982, and, though there was no legal necessity, it was agreed that a Faculty would only be applied for with the approval of the congregation. A majority of two-thirds was called for, but this target was not reached at the A.P.C.M. in 1983, though over half those present voted in favour.

The Council then decided that the removal of the screen should be part of a wider re-ordering of the interior, and a report was commissioned from the Revd. Professor J. G. Davies, Professor of Architecture and Theology at Birmingham University. His most radical proposal was to turn the Church interior round 180°, so that worship would have been in a westerly direction. The report was presented to the A.P.C.M. in 1987 and members of the congregation were invited to submit proposals of their own. Many were received, and plans were afterwards drawn up by Niall Patterson Associates.

The scheme won support from many in the congregation and the full cost of the proposed work (£146,000) was raised by voluntary contributions, but it was also opposed by other parishioners, and seventy two objections were lodged against the granting of a Faculty.

A Consistory Court, lasting three days, was held in the Church Hall before Chancellor H. H. Lomas in October 1988 and eloquent arguments were put forward by both sides. J.L.O. Holden, a collateral descendent of the Very Revd. John Nutter, Rector of Bebington (1581-1602) acted as Counsel for the petitioners, and the entire proceedings were recorded on seventeen tapes (which are kept in the Vestry safe).

View of re-ordered church

The majority of the changes for which the application was made were approved by the Chancellor. These included the carpeting of the aisles, angling the side pews to improve visibility, replacing the inner porch doors with glass doors, the removal of the chancel screen to the side of the vestry (where if forms a passage to the small door in the north east corner), the removal of the choir stalls (which were given to St . James, New Brighton), and the construction of a dais to create a ministry area in the Chancel. It was also agreed that the font at the west end could be re-sited, and that a staircase and upper room could be constructed in the tower, with a kitchen and lavatory below. However, the proposed alterations to the Feilden Chapel and the removal of the pulpit to the south wall were not authorised.

A new heating and lighting system was installed at this time, and the hatchments which had formerly hung in the tower were cleaned and re-hung in their present position on the north and south walls of the nave.

During the re-ordering the Church was closed and services were held in the Gladstone Theatre in Port Sunlight. It was re-opened on 25 June 1989, by the Rt. Revd. M.A. Baughen, Bishop of Chester.

THE TOWER

The masons' marks in the lower parts of the tower date from between 1300 and 1320 and those in the ringing loft are from the middle of the fourteenth century. It has a broach spire on a square base and is divided by strings into three stages. The lower stage has a large decorated window of simple early character set in a deeply splayed recess. The middle stage originally had a single loophole (with a window added in 1849), and the upper has plain decorated windows on each of the four sides. There are three tiers of spire lights set in the octagonal spire alternately facing the cardinal points. The quinches consist of bold arches below the receding faces, and there are heavy buttresses three feet wide which extend seven feet at the lower stage. The door to the tower from the outside was blocked in the eighteenth century when a new door was cut within the church, but was re-opened in 1847.

The tower, which was famous for its ivy, was struck by lightning in May 1805. The accounts for that year show the purchase of ropes, tackle, and scaffolding, and the payment of £151.6.6d to Thomas Francis and Job Yeardsley 'for taking down and re-building the steeple'. In 1867 the top of the spire was damaged in a gale and the Liverpool architect G.A. Audsley oversaw a second rebuilding. In 1905 the tower and steeple were again repaired and repointed. The weathercock and vane was regilded in 1805, 1868, and 1904, but was afterwards declared unsafe and removed.

The ivy grew from a large root in the corner where the door is sited, but in 1847, when the door was reopened, 'this emblem of eternity', as Reed called it in his article of 1848, was cut down. Some ivy remained growing round from the south side and by 1911 snow and rain on the creeper were (causing damage to the bell chamber. Louvres were then added to the small windows to prevent it entering the spire. A prophecy that the world would end when the ivy reached the vane is ascribed to

The Tower

Nixon, the Cheshire Prophet who is said to have lived during the reign of James I. None of his prophecies were printed before 1714 and none mention Bebington, but Egerton Leigh in 'The Legend of Bebington Spire' written for the *Ballads and Legends of Cheshire* in 1867 gives him the credit:

Hast thou heard what hast been said
  By seer Nixon, prophet dread?
Of Bebington's high-soaring spire
  Thus he spoke in words of fire.

'When that spire's vane shall clasp
  Ivy with its fatal grasp,
Then the last stern trumpet's call
  Live and dead shall summons all.'

Once it almost reached the height,
  Filling Cheshire with afright;
When the lightning's scorching blast,
  Through the threatening ivy past.

Twice since then in utmost need,
  Chance hath baulked the ivy's greed;
Still the tendrils seek the sky,
  Struggling towards the spire on high.

After the publication of this ballad the tradition took on the air of an old established legend. Philip Sulley in his work on *The Hundred of Wirral* (1889) refers to it as such and cites the earlier occasions on which the top of the steeple had collapsed as the ivy neared the vane. 'The creeper,' he said, 'is now nearing the summit again and its progress is watched with some interest by the older inabitants, who wonder whether nature will again interfere to prevent the consummation of the material half.'

Charles Reed refers to another popular belief concerning the tower: 'The most peculiar circumstance connected with this tower is the popular tradition and belief that it was the work of Inigo Jones, as well as the tower of the neigbouring church of Eastham, to which it certainly bears a remarkable similarity. I have endeavoured to ascertain the origin of this belief; and the worthy Rector, the Rev. R.M. Feilden, has told me he has seen documents that prove this; but these documents I have never been able to obtain a sight of. It is known that Inigo Jones had works in the neighbourhood, and an old Hall, a few miles off, is one of them.' Ormerod had mentioned Inigo Jones in connection with Eastham and discounted the tradition, but it spread to Bebington because of the similarity between the spires. Those who chose to believe the story overlooked the fact that Inigo Jones was born two hundred years after the tower was built.

THE BELLS

There were three bells at Bebington in 1549 according to the List of Church Goods in the Deanery of Wirral. These were recast in musical sequence in the seventeenth century and remained in use until the early nineteenth century. There are various references to them in the Church accounts. The first entry records 6/- paid to the ringers on 5th November 1774, and another the following year is for cleaning the bells. In 1785 John Goodacre was paid £1.3.6d for 27lbs of iron for 'mending the bell', and three times that amount was spent on the bells the following year. New bell ropes were a further regular expense. The sexton received 10/- for tolling the bell until 1809 when he was awarded an additional sum to sweep the pews and 'to Toll the Bell every Sunday at least Half an Hour before Morning and Evening service' and 'for a few Minutes when the Minister comes to his desk'.

The bell frame was badly decayed by 1825 and two of the bells had to be taken down. In 1845 a new peal of six bells was cast by George Mears and Company of the Whitechapel Bell Foundry. These weighed 26½cwt with a tenor bell of 6 cwt. 2qr. 24lbs. The belfry was cleaned and put in order in February 1846 and a special ceremony attended the first ringing of the bells. The original tenor bell was sold to the Reverend T.F. Redhead for use at St Peter's, Rock Ferry.

By 1906 the frame was again unsafe and a new one was installed the following year with provision for a complete peal of eight bells. William Watson, of Spital, gave a new treble and tenor bell, and the old fourth was recast a semitone lower to form the Fifth of the new octave. The work was again carried out by Mears and Stainbank and the new peal was dedicated on 12 August 1907. The eight bells weigh nearly 39 cwt -from the Tenor of 8 cwt 3qr. 10lbs (in G#, diameter 38") to the Treble of 3½cwt, and each is inscribed on the shoulder with the maker's name. The waist of the Fifth has 'Recast March 1907', and the Treble and Tenor are inscribed 'The gift of William Watson, High Sheriff of the County of Chester, March 1907'. At a Vestry meeting on 22 April 1908 it was decided that a brass plaque commemorating the new bells should be placed in the church. It is attached to the wall beyond the wooden screen leading to the rooms below the tower: 'In 1907 two bells the Gift of / Wm. Watson, J.P., D.L., of Spital / (High Sheriff of the County of Chester) / were added to the existing peal of six. / The whole eight bells having been hung in new / framework provided by Voluntary Contributions / were dedicated on August 12th, by the / Venerable Archdeacon Edward Barber.'

The first peal of 5,040 changes (eight bells rung 5,040 times and never twice in the same order) took place in September 1907. A stone tablet commemorating the ring was unveiled by the Rector in the belfry in September 1909, and is as follows:

Wirral Branch, Chester Diocesan Guild. A Peal of Grandsire Triples, 5040 changes, Carter's 12 part, rung on these bells, Saturday, September 7th, 1907, in 3 hours, 6 minutes, by

W. Burgess,	Treble	J. Cliff,	5th
J. Woods	2nd	*H. Hough,	6th
J. Shone	3rd	J. Dillon	7th
*J. Millington	4th	*E. Spencer	Tenor

*First peal. Also first peal of Triples for the Conductor, H.E. Hough.

First peal on the Bells after being augmented to eight by new Tenor and Treble, and an old fourth bell recast. Opened August 12th, 1907.

G.R. Feilden, M.A., Rector — J. Armstrong, B.M. Ormerod, Churchwardens.

Presented by Henry A. Marsh, Bebington.

The bells were re-tuned and refitted in 1975 by John Taylor of Liverpool, and in 1976 the volume of the peal was reduced by bricking up the louvres.

THE CHURCH VAULT

Until 1871 many burials took place in the church. The flagstones which made up the floor rested on the earth and the ground below was honeycombed with graves. It was more expensive than burial in the churchyard, but was deemed to be the more hallowed ground. In 1788 it was decreed that: 'Every Person who Buries in the Church shall pay to the Church Wardens the sum of Five shillings before they are suffered to disturb the Flags, and also to lay down the Flags again in a proper manner and repair other damages within 5 days after the Funeral, at their own expense or pay the further sum of Two Shillings and Sixpence to the Churchwardens for that purpose.'

The Rectors and neighbouring landowners were able to specify burial at the east end by the communion rails, but the main vault below the chancel was exclusive to the Lancelyns and Greens of Poulton Lancelyn whose right extended back to the earliest times. The names of those buried there in the seventeenth and eighteenth centuries are commemorated on the marble plaque by the altar. John Green who died in 1711 is among their number, and details of his burial are available from the account books in the library at Poulton Hall. These show that the funeral cost £52.7.5d, which included mourning linen, shoes, hats, black gloves, a copious supply of funeral baked meats, 28 bottles of claret, a supply of Canary wine, and cherry brandy. The other expenses were as follows:

Funerall Expenses, 1711	
Mony for ye Poor yn distributed	£ 3.00.00
pd. Mr Ludlow, Apothecary	5.01.06
pd. for Rosemary	2.00
pd. Morris Jones, Joiner, for ye Coffin	1.10.00
pd. Mr Wilkinson, Surgeon, for scering coffin	5.06.00
pd. Mr Holland for Cloth to cover ye coffin	14.06
Ralph Lyon, Coch man	5.00
pd. Mr Jones, Saddle & Pillion Cloth	5.00
Mr Hurt, Curate	1.01.06
to ye Sexton for ye Grave	5.00
pd. Mr Hall ye Parson for Burying in ye Chancell	1.00.00
pd. him for a Mortuary	10.00
pd. Mr Crompton for tolling ye Bell	5.05

Thomas Green was the last member of the family to lay absolute claim to the vault. He succeeded his grandfather, Richard, as Lord of the Manor in 1845, and when the church was restored the following year he took the opportunity to excavate and build a brick wall round four sides of the vault. His affidavit of 1889 gives details of the appearance and state of the vault at that time. He said that it extended up to the walls of the church and as far as the Communion rails (which were then at floor level running as far as the first pillar). Access was usually from the south-west corner. Six or seven lead coffins were temporarily removed and all were found to be in good order, and the interior was found to be dry. He added a new drain, paved the floor, and put in new beams for the roof. All the work was carried out at his own expense (over and above his contribution to the restoration which covered one third of the cost).

Thomas Green was living in Guernsey when the proposals for the restoration of 1871 were under discussion, and though his consent was asked for the abolition of his pews (of which he held the largest number and those closest to the pulpit), no mention was made of the family graves or the vault. When he visited the church after its restoration he found that the slabs round the altar had been moved to the north-east aisle as the altar had been raised on steps and the floor above tiled. Six years later the Rector applied for another Faculty to move the organ to the end of the north-east aisle where the stones had been relaid. At first Thomas Green opposed it, but he afterwards came to an amicable arrangement whereby (in the words of the *Chester Courant*) a 'brass plate would be placed on the wall in the chancel within the communion rails, bearing the inscription that in the vault below lay the remains of those persons whose names were on the tombstones which were now scattered about the church, and that the present stones should, as far as posible, be moved into the south side of the Poulton or Spital aisle'. He in due course provided the brass plate, but the stones were not returned to the floor of the church. They remained for many years in the churchyard and are now lost.

The matter was allowed to rest until 10 April 1888 when Thomas Green's son, [Thomas] Parnell Green died at Claughton in Lancashire (at the home of his uncle who was Rector). Thomas Green wanted the body to be buried in the family vault, but having failed to get the consent of the Rector attempted to claim his rights by other means. In 1889 he applied to the Consistory Court in Manchester for permission to exhume the body of his son (who had been buried at Claughton). He then applied to the Chancellor of the Diocese for a Faculty to permit the vault to be opened. He promised to have the body enclosed in a hermetically sealed coffin and either to lift and replace the floor tiles or to make a new entrance from outside. Everything would be done in the best possible way, entirely at his own expense and without danger to health.

The Rector, however, was opposed in principle to having any further burials within the church. A Parish Meeting was called on 23 September 1889, and as 'there was a general expression of disapproval of any internment taking place within the church' it was 'unanimously resolved to oppose the granting of the Faculty'. The two sides met at the Chancellor's Court in Chester Cathedral on 26 September but the meeting was adjourned. The matter was then argued at length before the Consistory Court on 28 November, but no final adjudication was to be made until the following year.

In a battle of wills, the Rector had powerful friends and they decided to bring the matter to the attention of the Home Office. Early in 1890 the Rector was able to announce that the Home Secretary intended to make an application for an Order of the Queen in Council for the discontinuance of burials within the church, and a notice to this effect was posted on the church door. It took effect on 1 May 1890, when by an Order of Her Majesty in Council it was decreed: 'That burials shall be discontinued forthwith and entirely within the Parish Church of Bebington, in the County of Chester.'

Thomas Green, who had come so close to winning his case, outlived the Rector by a few years and on his death in 1911 was buried in the new grave of the Lancelyn Greens on the south side of the church. By a curious quirk of fate the memorial given by his son (at the suggestion of the new Rector) was the altar which stands over the vault in which the coffins of his ancestors lie.

Other vaults or quasi-vaults may still remain under the floor, though most were dug up in 1871 when much of the floor was excavated to allow heating and ventilation to be installed below. The large number of bones which were unearthed at that time gave rise to the rumour that they were victims of the Battle of Brunenburgh (of AD937). Philip Sulley, in *The Hundred of Wirral* (1889) accepted this unlikely claim. 'Under the flooring,' he said, 'was found a large quantity of bones and skulls, many bearing evidence of wounds and violence, some even with fragments of iron and arrow heads imbedded, and numbers of arrow heads also. This would certainly point to a battle having been fought in the neighbourhood, and might be regarded as additional evidence of the great fight of Brunanburh.'

The other vaults most likely to survive would be on each side of the main vault under the north and south chapels. They would date back to the foundation of the building when the Lancelyns, the Mynshulls and the Chauntrells were able, as benefactors, to make provision for the vaults in which they would lie. According to Hugh Nicolson the unsanitary nature of the church before its restoration was caused by water flowing into the vaults and emitting an unpleasant smell: 'He told me,' wrote Hugh Edmund Boultbee, 'that when excavations were going on in connection with the Restoration, he saw a large Newfoundland dog slip into one of the vaults under the chancel which had been uncovered prior to concreting, and it began to swim round and round in the stinking water in a vain attempt to get out.'

THE HATCHMENTS

Hatchments were used as a pictorial announcement that a death had taken place in a family that bore arms. They were nailed to the wall of the house over the main entrance, and were then transferred to the church and offered up as a heraldic memorial. They are painted on canvas with plain wooden frames. The background indicates the status of the deceased, with the husband's arms on the dexter (the right hand side when held from behind, the left hand side when seen from the front), and those of the wife on the sinister. All black with a single coat of arms (as with Joseph Green) is for a bachelor. The dexter half painted black, the sinister half white (as with Richard Green) indicates that the deceased was a married man and was survived by his wife. The mottos are not those of the family, but ones appropriate to death.

The four hatchments in the Church were painted between 1826 and 1845, and were cleaned and restored in 1989.

ROGER JACSON [1826]

Hatchment of Roger Jacson

North aisle (between the windows): The Reverend Roger Jacson, A.M., Rector of Bebington, who married (1) Frances, daughter of the Reverend John Gibson, 1777; and (2) Mary Anton Johnson; died 6 March 1826, aged 72.

Dexter and centre background black. Quarterly 1st and 4th, Or a fess between sheldrakes proper (Jacson); 2nd, Gules a saltire between four annulets or (Shallcross); 3rd, Gules three lions rampant or (Fitzherbert), impaling two coats per pale, 1. Azure three storks rising argent (Gibson), 2. Or a chevron between three lions' heads erased or (Johnson). Crest: a sheldrake proper. Mantling: Gules and Argent. Motto: 'Resurgam'.

GEORGE ORRED, OF TRANMERE & HIGHER BEBINGTON [1828]

Hatchment of George Orrod

South aisle (between the windows): George Orred, Lord of the Manor of Tranmere and Higher Bebington, who married Frances, daughter of William Woodville, of Edge Hill, Lancashire (1803); died 19 December 1828.

All black background. Gules a fess dancetty argent (Orred), impaling, Quarterly, 1st and 4th, Argent a fess and a canton gules (Woodville), 2nd and 3rd, Argent a fess voided, on a canton gules a cross moline or. To dexter of main shield, Argent a cross engrailed gules, over all a bend azure (for Tranmere); to sinister of main shield, Sable three stags' heads cabossed argent (Bebington). Crest: a hare courant proper, bearing in its mouth three ears of corn. Mantling: Gules and argent. Motto: 'Hinc Orior'.

JOSEPH GREEN, OF POULTON LANCELYN [1829]

Hatchment of Joseph Green

North aisle (by doorway): Joseph (Kent) Green, Lord of the Manor of Poulton Lancelyn and Nether Bebington, born 1773, grandson of Catherine Kent (nee Green), assumed the name and arms of Green by royal sign manual (26 February 1793) in accordance with the will of Priscilla Parnell (daughter of John Green, of Poulton Lancelyn); died, unmarried, 8 April 1829.

A circular shield with decorative border. Azure three stags trippant or, on a chief or three crescents sable (Green). Crest: A demi-stag per fess or and azure charged with two crescents in pale counterchanged. Mantling: Gules and argent. Motto: 'Resurgam'. With a skull below.

RICHARD GREEN, OF POULTON LANCELYN [1845]

Hatchment of Richard Green

South aisle (by doorway): Richard (Kent) Green, of Poulton Lancelyn and Nether Bebington, who married Jane Henley, of London (1791); died 1845. Heir to his cousin, Joseph (above), on whose decease in 1829 he assumed the name and arms of Green in accordance with the terms of Priscilla Parnell's will.

Green, as for Joseph Green, but three stags or ermined sable, impaling. Paly of eight argent and gules (Henley). Crest: as above. Mantling: Very flowery, gilded. Motto: 'Resurgam'.

THE CHURCH PLATE

A list of Church Goods in the Deanery of Wirral in 1549 mentions two chalices, but neither has survived , nor has the silver salver for the communion which was given to the Church by Lady Leicester in 1668 (of which there is a record on the Benefactor's Board). The earliest plate is a Stand Paten of 1704-5, and two chalices by Richard Richardson of 1736 and 1769.

A GUIDE TO THE CHURCH

THE CHANCEL

The oldest fixtures in the chancel are the two inverted pyramid shaped semi-octagonal wall brackets on the side walls which were designed for lamps. The piscina (for washing vessels) on the south return is also contemporary with the structure. It has a four-centred moulded arch with a plain slab replacing the original bowl, and may once have shared the wall with an aumbry. The small doorway on the right of the altar was blocked in 1827, but partly revealed in 1897 when the lath and plaster was removed. It led to a vestry or sacristy built against the east wall.

The main east window was dedicated on 13 December 1953 and shows 'The Last Supper' and 'Christ the King' with other sacred symbols. The previous window which had German stained glass in memory of Miss Frances Feilden, the Rector's sister (who died in 1856), was destroyed in 1941 by a stray German bomb.

The carved altar was designed by Charles E. Deacon of Liverpool and carved by Harry Hems of Exeter. It was presented by Major Herbert Lancelyn Green in memory of his father. and is inscribed on the right hand side: 'Dedicated to the Glory of God, and to the Loving Memory of Thomas Green, of the Hall, Poulton Lancelyn, 1911'. It bears two texts on the front: 'Thou art the King of Glory, O Christ' and 'Thou art the Everlasting Son of the Father'. Major Green's daughter, Gwen, is thought to have been the model for the heads of the angels on the front. The Victorian altar table which it replaced was given to St. Mark's, New Ferry, for use in a side chapel.

The oak reredos (which replaced one given in 1863 in memory of Richard Mosley Feilden) was erected as a memorial to the Reverend Hugh Edmund Boultbee who served as Rector from 1918 to 1941. It was designed by Bernard A. Miller and made by L. Brown and Sons of Wilmslow, and was dedicated on 20 October 1951. The motifs on the panels are from left to right: the cross of St Andrew, the Arms of the Abbey of St Werburgh, the Arms of the See of Chester; a rebus on the name of 'Boultbee' (cross arrows or 'bolts' intersected by targets or 'bees'), the Arms of the Northern Province of York (where the Rector was ordained), I.S., and the arms of Durham University (at which the Rector took his degrees). The words of the Creed, the Lord's Prayer, and the Ten Commandments were added to the plain side panels in 1961.

The memorials within the rails of the sacrarium are for the Lords of the Manor of Poulton and Lower Bebington and for former Rectors and their families. On the north wall there is an imposing black and white marble

The Chancel

monument surmounted by an urn with drapery. It dates from 1793 and gives the names of the Greens of Poulton Lancelyn who are buried in the vault below:

PRISCILLA eldest sister and heiress of ED. GREEN, Esq.
widow of JOHN PARNELL Esqr. of Chester
died Decr. 18th, 1792 aged 86.
URSULA GREEN spinster died Decr. 1791 aged 84
ED. PARNELL Esq. Son of JOHN & PRISICILLA
died unmarried Aug. 1776 aged 39.
ELIZH. GREEN spinster died May 1751 aged 44.
Within these rails their remains are deposited
With those of numerous ancestors
resident at Poulton Lancelyn in this Parish
for more than seven centuries
and Lords also of this Manor
The Righteous shall be had
in everlasting remembrance.

The ornate canopied niche in the corner dates from the sixteenth century. The original statue (either of St Andrew or the Virgin Mary) was removed in the seventeenth century and the present statue of St. Andrew is modern. It was placed here in May 1917 by the Rector in memory of his son who was killed on St. Andrew's Day (30 November) 1915. The granite tablet on the adjacent wall is: 'To the Glory of God / And in grateful and loving memory of / Kenneth George Haslam Ford (O.M.) / Lieut. and Machine Gun Officer The Cheshire Regt. / Eldest Son of the Ven. G.A. Ford, Rector of this Parish. / Who fell in France St Andrew's Day 1915 / and is buried at Bailleull / The figure of St Andrew was restored by his family / "He died while carrying out a dangerous duty / like the fearless lad he was."

To the right of the east window there is a stone memorial with pediment: 'SACRED TO THE MEMORY OF / ROGER JACSON A.M. / NEARLY FIFTY YEARS RECTOR OF THIS PARISH, / A MAGISTRATE FOR THE COUNTY, / AND FORTY YEARS CHAIRMAN OF THE QUARTER SESSIONS, / HE DIED THE SIXTH OF MARCH 1826 IN HIS SEVENTY-THIRD YEAR: / BELOVED, REVERED, AND MOST DEEPLY LAMENTED. / PRACTICAL RELIGION / WAS THE GUIDE OF HIS EMINENTLY USEFUL LIFE: / HE TAUGHT HER PRECEPTS PURE AND UNDEFILED. / AND IN HIMSELF EXEMPLIFIED / HOW CHEERING AND HOW SOCIAL ARE HER PATHS.'

A brass tablet below has the crest and motto of the Lancelyn Green family and was erected in 1878. It refers to the family graves which were within the altar rails: 'Certain / tombstones from the places / used during nearly eight centuries / for the sepulture of the Lancelyns / and Greenes the descendants of Siward / the donor of Bebington Church to / St Werburgh's Abbey, A.D. 1093. / having been removed from the Chancel this / Brass is placed here to certify the fact by / Thomas Green of Poulton Lancelyn / A.D. 1878.' The tombstones were moved during the restoration of 1871 when marble steps and tiles replaced the old flagstones.

The unusual clerestory window on the south return, which allowed light to fall on the canopied figure in the opposite corner, has a transom with elliptic arches at the head and foot. Below it there is a pyramidal monument of black and white marble (with the head of an angel at the base).

This is: 'In Memorey of / Edward Green Esquire / only Son of Iohn Green Esqr / by Priscilla his Wife / dyed Without Issue / May 19th. 1756 / Aged 50.' He was the last direct male heir of the Greens of Poulton Lancelyn and was succeeded by his sister, Priscilla, whose memorial is on the facing wall. Beneath it again there is small brass plate in memory of Siward Richard Lancelyn Green, the second son of Major Gilbert and Phyllis Green of Poulton Lancelyn, who died in March 1936, at the age of 11.

Parish Chest

The parish chest which stands to the left of the altar dates from the early sixteenth century and was used to store the Parish Registers, church plate, and vestments. It has legs and iron strap hinges, and was designed with three locks. The keys were held by the Rector and the Churchwardens and the chest could only be opened when all were present. It was replaced by an iron chest in 1818 and by a 'Milner's Patent Safe' in 1847 (built into the wall of the Tower vestry). A free standing safe was purchased in 1885 when the vestry was moved to the north-east corner of the church.

The Bishop's throne is Jacobean and is a fine example of its type. Next to it there is a small throne made from two carved poppyhead bench ends. It was constructed in 1897. Two other chairs of a similar design were made in 1989 when the choir stalls were removed. The bench ends have poppy head finials with intricate Perpendicular tracery. As well as the six in the church, there is one other which has suffered from woodworm in the heating chamber below the north aisle.

The three stalls on the south or epistle side of the altar are for the use of the celebrants of the Communion or for the deacon and subdeacons (and together they make up a movable version of the stone 'sedilia' found in early churches). The group is constructed from the arms and seats of the main stalls. There were originally twelve of these seats, possibly surmounted by canopies, and they were designed to stand between the arcades (where the parclose screens now are). Six survived until 1847 though they were badly affected by damp and dry rot. They were made up into two pairs in 1871 and were remade in their present form in 1897. The stalls are separated by high curved elbows and have folding seats with 'misericords' on the underside. The mediaeval carving is very fine. The first has a pelican, the next a group of fish, and the third a portrait head. Other pieces of wood from the early benches and pews were re-used in the panelling of the north porch.

THE SOUTH OR FEILDEN CHAPEL

The end of the south aisle was designed for use as a chapel and there are two lamp brackets on either side of the altar and an aumbry on the right which date from the sixteenth century. There are also several ancient slabs which have been set in a row below the bottom step of the altar. The first is dated 1787 with the initials 'M.H.' and another alongside has part of an inscription with the date 'August 1720'. The older grave slabs (from the sixteenth and seventeenth century) were originally in the chancel. These have crosses on a curved base (representing Mount Calvary). A sword or dagger was for a man, and shears were

The Misericords

for a woman. The ones which survive were used to repair the east wall behind the altar and were moved to their present position in 1908. One has a foliated cross resting on a curved base; another has the head of a cross, and a third shows a sword hilt and dagger. Other similar fragments survive elsewhere in the church. One with a cross on three steps with a sword was built into the wall of the heating chamber in 1847; another fragment with the trefoiled head of a cross was placed over the south nave arcade, and a third is embedded in the wall of the churchyard. The best preserved is set into the north wall and was for a child. The indistinct inscription 'HW 1555' which was placed over the entrance to the north porch in 1847 may also be an early memorial.

A blocked doorway at the east end of the south wall once gave access to the Poulton and Storeton aisle and to a small vestry which was built in the corner in the early nineteenth century. The door was closed in 1847 and the wall made good, but the frame outside is still visible and the door itself was left in place until it decayed.

The earliest memorial in the south chapel is the black stone monu - ment on the left of the window. It commemorates the Lords of the Manor of Poulton and Lower Bebington who were buried in the north chapel and chancel. It was first erected at the east end of the North aisle in 1742 and was moved to its present position in 1878. It is surmounted by a stag and has conventional palms and scrolls with the Arms of the Greens of Poulton Lancelyn (Azure, three stags trippant Or; Crest, on a wreath, with a demistag salient Or). Below are the words: 'Near this / are Interred in Hope / of a Blefsed Refurrection / *thro' JESUS CHRIST our LORD*/ the Bodys of the GREENS / of POOLTON LANCELYN, Esqrs. / Viz. / Edward, 1631. Randle, 1639. / Henry, 1653, Richd, *jan* 1677. / His Wife Ursula, Daughter to / Sr. Thos. Bunbury, Bart. May 1678. / Edward, 1694. John, 1711 / His Wife Priscilla, Decr_•. 15th 1749. / The Revd. Thos. Green, jan. 17th / 1746 / [*on the base*] Thos. Green, A.M. Rr of WOOODch erected this / 1742.'

The neighbouring manor of Tranmere and Higher Bebington is represented by the memorials of the Orred family. Near the lamp bracket on the left are two small brass plaques (from grave slabs on the floor) to Stanley Orred of the Woodside in Sutton 'who departed this Life on the 25th May 1771 / In the 42nd year of his Age', and to his wife, Ann (*nee* Okell, who brought the Woodside estate as her dowry) 'who died May 28th. 1799 in the 64th Year of her Age'. A copper tablet under the window sill on the right (also from a grave slab) is in memory of their second son: 'Here lies the Remains of / Daniel Son of Stanley and / Ann Orred of Sutton / who departed this life / October 26th, 1783 / in the 27th Year of his Age.' Stanley Orred was the eldest son of George Orred of

Tranmere (born 1704) by his wife Margaret. The large marble memorial set at an angle on the right of the altar bears the arms of the Orred family with crossed torches below, and is in memory of three members of the Orred family: Daniel Orred, of the City of Chester (the fourth son of George Orred by his second wife Anne), who died without issue on 29 June 1826, aged 85; George Orred, of Aigburth whose hatchment hangs in the south aisle (the son of Fletcher Orred of Bebington and elder brother of Daniel), who died on 19 December 1828, aged 59; and his wife, Frances (the daughter of William Woodville of Liverpool), who died on 1 July 1825, aged 54. There are several other memorials in the churchyard, including a cenotaph for George Orred, the son and heir of George and Frances Orred, who died at Lucerne on 27 October 1869, aged 62.

Three small heart shaped brass tablets with skull and bone devices (on the left of the altar) are from the graves of the Cromptons, the father and son who in the eighteenth century served as schoolmaster and Parish Clerk at Bebington: '*Interred here / THOMAS CROMTON / the Elder /* Novr. the 5th / 1719.'; '*Alice / Wife /* OF Thos. CROMPTON / *was [here] interred /* Decemr. 11th. / 17 ... 24'; 'Thomas *Cromton / died 11th* Janry 1791. Aged 90. Yrs.'

Two early brass plaques from gravestones are attached to the wall on the right of the altar. One in Latin (with a Hebrew text below) comes from the floor of the chancel and is from the grave of Ralph Poole who succeeded his father, Hugh, as Rector of Bebington in 1647 and died on 5 April 1662:

RADVLPHVS POOLE HVGONI PATRI
TAM SVGGESTO QVAM SEPVLCHRO
EODEM SVCCESSOR COLLECTVS
FVIT AD PATRES APRILIS 7
1662.

The other is taken from the grave of William Glover (whose name is also found among the list of Benefactors): 'HERE LYETH THE BODY / OF WILLIAM GLOVER / OF LOWER BEVINGTON / WHO WAS BURYED NOVEM / BER: 23: ANNO DOM: 1692'.

A further brass plaque bears the name of Andrew Tucker Squarey, of Gorsey Hey, Bebington, who died on 29 April 1900. He was the attorney and later solicitor to the Mersey Docks and Harbour Board. He served on many committees concerned with the restoration and improvement of the church and provided the crosses which adorn the western gables.

The other memorials, furnishings, and fittings are to Robert and George Feilden, the Victorian Rectors of Bebington. The brass plaque below the bracket to the left of the altar (which was moved from under the window in 1908) is inscribed in red and black: 'In memory of the / Reverend Robert Mosley Feilden, M.A. / Rector for 36 years of the Parish of Bebington, / and Chairman for a long period of the Bench / of Magistrates, for the Hundred of Wirral, / who died May 14th, 1862, aged 67 years, / and was buried in the adjoining ground. / This window and the Reredos were erected by / his Parishioners, Brother-Magistrates and Friends.' The German stained glass to which it refers was destroyed in the Blitz in 1941 and the Victorian altar reredos behind the main altar was replaced in 1951.

The altar, reredos, furniture, and the transept and parclose screens (including those across the north aisle and arcade) date from 1908 when the end of the south aisle was converted into a Lady Chapel in memoryof Canon Feilden, who died on 13 October 1907. The chapel was dedicated on 6 January 1909 by the Dean of Chester. The designs are by C.E. Deacon and Horsburgh and the work was executed by Harry Hems of Exeter. The screen across the entrance to the chapel is inscribed: 'TO THE GLORY OF GOD AND IN // MEMORY OF GEORGE RAMSAY FEILDEN, FOR 45 YEARS RECTOR // OF THIS PARISH . THIS CHAPEL IS FURNISHED & THESE // SCREENS ERECTED BY HIS FAMILY, PARISHIONERS & FRIENDS.'

The oak altar and reredos were given by the Feilden family. The figures under the canopies represent St George, St Margaret, St Catherine and St Mark and are in honour of George Feilden, his wife, Margaret, and the daughter churches, of St Catherines's, Tranmere, and St Mark's, New Ferry. Other individual gifts made at the time include the brass cross, candlesticks, credence table, and Book Desk (made or supplied by Harold Stabler), an Alms Dish, Bible, a silver chalice, and a paten. The steps below the altar, the new communion rails, the seating, gas pendants, rugs, carpets and kneelers, the wine and water flagons, the hymn books, and the screens themselves were paid for by voluntary subscriptions. The backs of the two chairs are carved. One has three wheatsheaves for the County of Cheshire, and the other has the arms and motto of the Feilden family ('Virtutis Praemium Honor'/'Honour is the first of Virtues'). The Eagle reading desk which stands in the corner is contemporary with the pulpit and was given by Harmood W. Banner in 1873.

There are three memorials below the windows on the south wall. The earliest is an ornate bronze in the third bay: 'In grateful memory of Mary Platt and of 40 years of loving and devoted service in the family of George Ramsay Feilden / Died February 20th 1908'. The second is an oval plaque by the altar in memory of George Augustus Feilden, the Rector's youngest son, who died at Fairlie, New Zealand on 23 June 1914, aged 43. And the third is a small brass plate in memory of three further members of the family: the Rector's eldest son, Ramsay Robert Feilden (18671956); his daughter, Ursula Margaret Feilden (1869-1954); and a grandson, Ramsay George Feilden (1902-75) - the son of George Augustus Feilden. The present east window dates from 1954 and has coats of arms in the second and fourth lights. Those on the left are for the Diocese of Chester (the three mitres) and for the Borough of Bebington (comprising a white St Andrew's cross for Bebington, a ship for Eastham, rays for Port Sunlight, the Bromborough cross, and the motto 'Civitatis Fortuna'). Those on the right are for the County of Cheshire (the three wheatsheaves) and for the Feilden family (crest and motto). Remnants of highly coloured glass with coats of arms remain in the small top lights of the perpendicular windows on the side walls, and the windows below are filled with plain Victorian glass, with patterned borders.

The banner closest to the altar is the colour of the Cheshire Regiment and a plaque on the adjacent pillar gives its history: 'This Colour of the 2nd Garrison Battalion / The 22nd (Cheshire) Regiment / Presented in 1921, was laid up within these / sacred walls by Major K.J. Beardwood / on Armistice Day, Nov. 11, 1934 / This Battalion was formed in 1915 and / worshipped here prior to serving / overseas during the Great War'.

THE SOUTH WALL:

The stained glass in the two perpendicular windows on either side of the screen in the south aisle was designed by Henry Holiday (1839-1927) and made by James Powell and Sons of the Whitefriars Glassworks in London (the same team who in 1880 designed and made the windows for St Mark's, New Ferry). The window beyond the screen represents Holy Women of the Old and New Testaments, with Sarah, Hannah, Ruth, and Esther in the upper lights, and the Virgin Mary, Elizabeth, Mary of Bethany, and Dorcas in the lower. It was unveiled on Easter Day 1881 and was given by William Rodger, of Oaklands, Spital in memory of his wife. The glass is inscribed: 'To the Glory of God and in Loving / Memory of Sarah Rodger / who entered into rest / 3rd July 1880 Aged 64 Years'. The second window (within the chapel) dates from 1886 and depicts Holy Men of the Bible, with Abraham, Moses, David, and Elijah in the upper lights, and St Peter, St Matthew, St Andrew, and St John in the lower. Plaques on the window ledges are: 'To the Glory of God / and in Loving Memory / of William Rodger who died / October 28th 1885 Aged 76 Years.' These windows are contemporary with and similar in

The Henry Holiday windows

design to those which Henry Holiday made for the south choir of Salisbury Cathedral. They also show Holy Women (with Sarah, Hannah, Ruth, Esther and the four Marys) and Holy Men (St Joseph the Carpenter, St James, St John, St Joseph, Jacob, Moses, Joshua, and Solomon) and were erected in memory of Mary, Countess of Radnor (1880) and the 4th Earl of Radnor (1891).

Below the Holiday windows and on the wall beyond are four memorials to men who fought in the Great War: a brass tablet to Herbert Percy Parry, the son of William and Jane Parry, who was killed in France on 1 July 1916; a slate and marble memorial surmounted by the insignia of the Cheshire Regiment to Herbert Allan Brown, a Private in the 13th Battalion who 'for many years sang in this choir' and was killed at the Battle of Ypres on 8 June 1917 (erected 1924); a brass plate in honour of 2nd Lieutenant Richard Powell Scholefield, the son of Henry and Elizabeth Scholefield, of Poulton Hey, who fought with the Cheshire Regiment and died in France on 25 July 1916 (erected 1917); and a marble tablet to Leslie Russell Alcock Gatehouse, of Abbot's Grange, who died on 3 October 1926 from wounds sustained at Givenchy on 9 April 1918 (erected 1928).

The Hatchment of George Orred who died in 1828 hangs above the memorials, and that of Richard Green who died on 8 April 1845 is to the right of the next window.

The stained glass in the small window dates from 1898 and is by Clayton and Bell. It shows St Martin clothing a beggar and is in memory of Henry Barton Wignall, of Woodhey, Spital, who died on 29th March 1897. It was given by his children and was unveiled on the first anniversary of his death. A brass plaque below the sill explains the subject: 'S. Martin, a Roman Soldier, A.D. 332, meeting a half naked beggar, in severe winter weather, cut off half of his own cloak with his sword and gave it to him; the following night he saw a vision of our Lord wearing the parted cloak, and saying to his attendant angels "Know ye who hath arrayed Me thus? My servant Martin hath done this." Fragments of early frescoes (which once covered the Norman walls) survive round the doorway leading to the south porch. 'The patterns seem to have been entirely foliated work, in chocolate and black upon a white ground,' wrote Edward Cox in 1898, soon after the plaster and whitewash had been removed and the frescoes revealed: 'There is a running pattern round the window openings and the doorway, and the wall spaces were treated with undulating and spiral stems, with leaves formed like those of a willow.' Other remnants (some coloured red and yellow) were uncovered on the west wall including 'a helmed head, with a serpent crest' which Cox thought might represent St Michael overthrowing Satan.

To the right of the porch (above a chair made from the ends of the Tudor choir stalls) there is an alabaster plaque given by Hugh Nicholson in memory of his father, Hugh Hathorn Nicholson, of Spital Hall, a 'constant worshipper' and generous benefactor, who died on 7 February 1929 at the age of ninety-nine. Next to it there is a granite memorial to Bernard Mackenzie Ormerod which was erected in 1931. This is surmounted by the badge of the Church Lads' Brigade and bears the following inscription: 'Lest we forget Bernard Mackenzie Ormerod. Born 14th August 1873 - Died 27th November 1927, who for 11 years served as Churchwarden of this Parish. A founder of the Bebington Company of the Church Lads' Brigade. He built the Drill Hall for its use and at the time of his death was its honoured and beloved Colonel, having spent at least half of his short life in loving service for the young manhood of the district. This tablet has been erected to his memory by members of this Church together with past and present members of his Company.' The plaque complements the epitaph on his grave: 'His heart was with the young manhood of Bebington, for whom he expended his time and energy. He was a loyal citizen, a loving friend and a Christian Gentleman.'

A Benefactors' Board hangs to the right of the high-silled window and gives the names and bequests of three Victorian benefactors, John Fitchett, Thomas Francis, and Richard Jones.

THE WEST END

The base of the tower which was formerly used as a vestry was converted during the re-ordering of 1989. An angled staircase leads to an upper room or creche with glass doors, and there are lavatories and a small kitchen below which are separated from the body of the church by an oak screen. A plaque made by T.J Thomason and Son, of Birkenhead (on the wall within the screen) commemorates William Watson's gift of two new bells in 1907. A plaque under the staircase is 'In Memory of Mary Elizabeth Sarsfield who died on the 15th March 1926'. It was erected 'as a grateful record of her generous bequest of £1,200 to the Funds of the Bebington Home Mission'. The Mission was founded in 1891 and its objects were re-defined in 1929 on the strength of this bequest as being for the benefit of the Women's Meeting and the relief of the poor. The legacy was used to assist the annual Women's Fellowship Outing and Christmas Party, and to provide pensions.

There is an unidentified wooden fragment below the plaque which resembles the cross bar of a chair and has the initials 'W.B.' and the date '1661' carved upon it. High above the Sarsfield plaque there is a large wooden board with the 'Catalogue of Benefactors to ye Parish of Bebington'. It dates from the beginning of the eighteenth century. The first twelve bequests from 1620 to 1698 are in one hand, while the last two for 1711 and 1728 were added after the bequests had been made.

The base of the tower at the West End

The Norman font is beyond the staircase and stands in the angle against the pillar. It dates from the 12th Century and is contemporary with the south wall and the nave arcade. The bowl is circular and made of white stone. It has a fillet under the rim with a row of open depressions, and there are six plain side panels of unequal size below. It stands on an octagonal base which is thought to be of a later date and originally had a high conical wooden cover. The font was in continuous use until the early nineteenth century when it was replaced by a 'quasi font' which stood in the north-east corner of the church. (The new font was discarded

The Font

in 1847 and taken to the garden of Bebington Hall where it was used as a fountain. It may then have been moved to the grounds of the Bromborough Rectory where an identical 'quasi font' served as a sundial.) The Norman font never left the church but was concealed when the gallery was built in 1829. It came back into use after the gallery was demolished in 1847 and the old cover or a new one in the gothic manner was placed over it with a hoist to enable it to be lifted. A drawing of the church at the time shows a rope passing over three pulleys: one attached to the beam immediately above, another in the angle of the roof, and a third fixed to the arcade wall. In 1871 the font was moved to the west end of the central aisle, and as it was impossible to fix the pulleys to the roof the cover was discarded. The font was moved to its present position in the re-ordering of 1989. The present wooden lid dates from 1871 and is flat with an iron ring in the centre. It was based on the early font lids which were fixed with staples and padlocked to prevent theft of the Holy Water.

To the right of the font and above the wardens' pews there is a small shelf. The carving of a suckling pig used as the bracket comes from one of the old misericords. Nearby there is the long narrow lid of a poor box (with a hinged opening with slot and keyhole) on which there is 'A Catalogue of Benefactors to ye Poor of Bebington, for Bread'. The names are listed in three columns, thus:

AD		£
1641	THOMAS CLEAVE, LONDON	50.
1664	JOHN SMITH, STORETON	10.
1668	LADY LEICESTER, SILVER SALVER COMMUNION	
1693	JOHN ECCLES, TRANMERE	40
1694	EDWARD GREEN, ESQR. POULTON	10
1698	RICHARD CARTER, BRIMSTAGE	20
1711	JOHN GREEN, ESQR. POULTON	10
1728	RICHARD YOCKSON, TRANMERE POOR	100
1839	JOHN FITCHETT, BEBINGTON	50
1847	THOMAS FRANCIS, BEBINGTON	100
1859	R. JONES, BEBINGTON...........PEW 23	& 20

To the right there is the carved Bread Board of 1641 which is inscribed:

IF HM CW

50.0.0 FOR BREAD

APRILL: 23

THE GIFT OF MR. THO. CLEAVE

CITIZEN OF LONDON AN: DO. 1641.

Loaves of bread were placed on this shelf and were distributed after the Sunday service by the churchwardens. The initials at the top are for John Fairclough ('IF') and Henry Meols ('HM'), Church Wardens ('CW'). The carved boss below is taken from another misericord.

The old west window originally had two lights, but was enlarged to three in 1884 (and for this reason is slightly off centre). The stained glass was made by Forrest and Bromley and shows St Peter, St Andrew, and St Paul. Four Evangelists were ordered in 1847 for the two west windows. The St John, however, was in reverse, as Charles Reed pointed out in his article of 1848: 'three of them have the left hand holding books, whilst St John has his pen likewise in his left hand, the artist having forgotten to make his drawings in reverse.' The problem was solved when the west window was enlarged, as it was logical to reinstate three figures and discard the one which had given offence. The west window at the end of the north aisle from which the glass came was filled with decorative floral glass similar to that used in the reconstructed windows nearby. Reed disliked the highly ornate patternbook glass used in these windows, and when the remaining windows in other parts of the church were reglazed in 1854 and 1861, Forrest and Bromley supplied a plainer edged glass.

Below the window at the west end of the north aisle there is a large arched tomb: SACRED / to the Memory of / The Revd JAMES NEWTON of *West Kirby*, who / departed this life at *Upper Tranmere* 16th August 1829. / Aged 74 Years. / Also in memory of MARTHA Relict of the said Revd / James Newton, who died at *Upper Tranmere* 20th March / 1833, Aged 80 Years.' James Newton was Curate of West Kirby from 1780-1822, and was buried at Bebington on 22 August 1829.

To the right of the monument there is a grey and white marble memorial (moved from the old north aisle in 1847): 'In Memory of / WILLIAM, Son of RICHARD WORRALL, of Tranmere, / who died 14th Oct. 1732, aged 10 Years. / RICHARD WORRALL, who died 14th May 1741, / aged 11 Years. / WILLOUGBY, baptized 29th April 1737. / JOHN, died 31st May 1741 / HANNAH died 13th June 1741, aged 10 months / Also RICHARD WORRALL, died 24th July 1742 / And DOROTHY widow of RICHARD WORRALL died / 12th July 1785, aged 90 years / SAMUEL SALISBURY Esq. died the 22nd Dec 1796, / Aged 72 years.'

THE NORTH WALL

A tablet at the west end of the north wall (moved from a pillar in 1847) is in memory of John Jacson, the twin brother of Roger and son of the Reverend Robert Jacson, Rector of Bebington: 'A.M. / Johs. Rev. R.

Jacson / Filii nat: max / Ob. Mar. 6 1799 AET 20 / By the exercise of chearful Piety / and really Christian Resignation / Thro'out a painful illness / of Seven years continuance / He learn'd the two great leffons / How to *live* & how to *die* / To our grief alafs, but his own / *IMMORTAL HAPPINESS* / He was appointed to the Practice / Only of the *Latter*.'

Below the memorial to Robert Jacson, there is another erected by Edward Martineau (a Liverpool merchant) as 'a humble but affectionate tribute' to his wife, Eleanor, the daughter of Edward Rogers, Esq. of Everton, who died on 14 December 1826 at the age of 33:

Cold in the dust the perished heart may lie,
But that which warmed it once shall never die
That spark unburied in its mortal frame.
With living light, eternal, and the same
Shall beam on Joy's interminable years
Unveiled by darkness - unassuaged by tears.

To the right of the window and the left of the North Porch there is an oak 'Roll of Honour' designed by Charles Deacon and made by Harry Hems of Exeter. It was dedicated on 14 October 1923 after the unveiling of the War Memorial and records the names of the seventy-three men from Bebington 'who died in the Great War to whose honour the cross in the Churchyard has been erected'.

Another board, erected in 1931, hangs to the right of the porch and gives a list of the Rectors of Bebington since 1286. The hatchment above bears the arms of Joseph Green, of Poulton Lancelyn, who died on 8 April 1829.

A small grave slab with an eight-armed cross in relief and incised shears (for a girl) is fixed to the wall below the next window. It was taken from the floor and fixed here in 1847 when the north aisle was extended. The hatchment of the Reverend Roger Jacson who died in 1826 hangs on the wall nearby, above three brass memorials. The first is to William and Eleanor Sinclair of Rock Ferry (who died in 1896 and 1906); the second is to Francis Edwin Sinclair, a Captain in the Royal Artillery (who died at Poonah, Bombay on 18 April 1889, aged 32) and also to Harold Sinclair (who died in 1887); and the third is in memory of Henry Burton Hassall, of Powycke, Spital (who died on 23 October 1883, aged 65) and of his wife, Anne (who died at Abbot's Grange in 1897).

The stained glass in the window of the north transept was designed by M. Warrington in 1859 and made by William Wailes of Newcastle. It was given by John Bolton Case, of Poulton Hey, and is inscribed in Latin to

Small grave slab

the memory of his parents, John Deane and Annabella Case: 'In Memoriam Johannis D. Case / et Annabella uxoris eius / hanc fenestram poni curaverunt / consanguinei superstites 1859.' The upper lights show scenes from the parable of the Good Samaritan with quotations from St Luke's gospel; and the lower have scenes from the Raising of Lazarus with quotations based on the Gospel of St John.

A brass plaque below is in memory of Margaret Storey, wife of the William Neale Clay, who died on 25 December 1885, and of her daughter, Frances, who died in 1903.

THE NORTH CHAPEL [VESTRY]:

The screen at the entrance to the Vestry was installed in 1908 as part of the memorial to Canon Feilden, and within there is the old chancel screen which he gave to the church in 1898 and which was moved here in 1989 to create a passage to the door in the north wall. The doorway itself was re-opened in 1909 when the new vestry was built. The oak cupboards and fittings are the gift of Thomas and Alice Oakshott who provided a hundred pounds to mark their Golden Wedding, and there is a small plaque attached to one set of drawers: 'To the Honour and Glory of God / and in thankful remembrance of the manifold / blessings during 50 Years of married life. / These Vestry Fittings are placed here by / Thomas William & Alice Eleanor Oakshott / of Derby House, Rock Ferry. / 19th August 1908.'

The floors are now carpeted and many of the gravestones of the Greens of Poulton Lancelyn and of other prominent people were removed when the church was refloored in 1871, but two slabs could still be seen in this part of the church early this century. One near the north-east door had the words: HERE LYETH / THE BODY OF / CAPT.-- WILLI / AM LANGFORD / DESEASED IAN / NUARY: I: 1654 (confirming a request made in his will of 13 December 1654 that his body should be buried in Bebington Church); and another was inscribed: 'E.G. 1694'. This was for Edward Greene, of Poulton Lancelyn, who was buried in the family vault on 15 March 1694.

The window at the east end of the north aisle was restored in 1844. Plain glass has replaced the Victorian stained glass, given in memory of the three children of J.B. Spence, which was destroyed in the Blitz. The glass in the north windows corresponds to that in the south windows with coloured glass in the top lights and edged Victorian glass below. The east wall under the window was refaced when the door on the chancel side was blocked and there is now no evidence of the two stone lamp brackets which were on either side of the space once filled by an altar. The wall is rough and the window plain because they were concealed by the large Victorian organ.

The present organ was built in 1962 by Henry Willis IV, of Henry Willis and Sons, Ltd. It has a plain oak casing and is constructed on stilts to allow light from the windows to reach the body of the church. There is a detached console with two manuals and fifteen stops: five each for the Great, Swell, and Pedal Organ. The keys are ivory and ebony, with the stops and couplers controlled by tilting ivory tablets. The concave pedalboard and console rest on a raised platform to allow the organist to see into the nave.

Before the church possessed an organ, the music was supplied by a small orchestra or band which included a bassoon and violoncello. The bassoon was hired in 1796 and thereafter the church accounts show the purchase of reeds and strings at regular intervals. Bebington had its own group of singers, and the church also played host to singers from other districts such as Heswall and Liverpool. The first singing master of whom there is a record is mentioned in the early 'Register of Banns' where there is a memorandum of an agreement made on 15 April 1796 between the parishioners and Benjamin Smith, singing master, 'the latter to attend the church on twelve Sundays for which he will be paid £3'. He did not stay long, but others were employed from time to time, and in 1833 the singing master was being paid £12 for six months' attendance. The singers performed at St Andrew's, St Catherine's, Tranmere, and at other neighbouring churches.

The first organ was installed in 1839 in a small gallery over the south aisle. Access was by means of a high level door cut through the south wall and approached by a flight of stone steps. It was dedicated on 1 April 1839, and the cost of the organist, singers, and organ blower (£17 in all) was defrayed by voluntary contributions from the pew owners. In the restoration of 1846-7 the organ was dismantled by J. Fleetwood and then resited at the west end of the new north aisle. In the restoration of 1871 it was taken to Chester by C. & J. Whitelely for cleaning and repair, and was afterwards placed in the centre of the west wall. A proposal for its transfer to the north-east aisle in 1878 proved impossible because of the lack of funds. It was also by then in very poor condition because of the damp and rot and it became virtually unplayable by 1882 though an attempt was made to repair it.

The prospectus for a new organ was issued in December 1883 and the work was entrusted to the Liverpool organ builder, E. Frankland Lloyd in May 1884. There was a service of dedication and a recital by the precentor of Chester on 11 February 1885. The 'huge and overpoweringly noisy organ', as Edward Cox described it, filled much of the north chapel with large pipes of 'spotted metal' on the west and south side. The console backed onto the choir and had three manuals and forty stops. It was worked 'on pneumatic principles' with a hand pump until 1896 when a 'hydraulic blowing mechanism' was added. It was overhauled by the maker in 1906 and was rededicated on 14 September 1950 after it had been restored and rebuilt.

The choir replaced the singers in 1862. The choristers sat at the base of the organ at the west end of the church until 1877. They then moved to the choir stalls in the nave, and were given surplices for the first time in 1879.

THE CHURCHYARD:

The Lychgate serves as a memorial to Clarke Aspinall (1827-91) and was dedicated on 2 September 1893. It was designed by Charles E. Deacon and built by Brown and Backhouse of Liverpool. The base is of Storeton stone, the main structure of English oak, and the roof of Ruabon tiles. The central cross beam is inscribed: 'To the Glory of God / And in Memory of Clarke Aspinall / for 35 years Churchwarden of this Parish / Erected by voluntary contributions / A.D. 1893'; and the cross bar facing the road bears the words: 'Look for the Resurrection of the Dead'. There are intricately carved panels on the gable front and provision has been made for these to be repeated on the churchyard side.

Near the North Porch (which was moved outwards when the Tranmere aisle was extended in 1847) there is the base of the cross with three of the original four octagonal sandstone steps. It may date from 1554 when the Bishop of Chester at his Visitation ordered the Churchwardens of Bebington 'to amend the churchyard and set up the crucifix before the feast of St Michael under penalty of xx shillings'. The head and shaft were taken down and buried in 1643 in compliance with an act of Parliament against 'Monuments of Superstition or Idolatry'. Part of the plinth (which Nathaniel Hawthorne mistook for an 'ancient baptismal font' in 1853) could still be seen last century. It had moulded bases for angle shafts round a central socket and there were carvings on the side panels. Grave digggers also retrieved a section of the head of the cross with carvings of the crucifixion and the Virgin and Child in rough niches under ogee foliated arches.

An earlier fourteenth century cross stood on the south side of the church. The base and part of the shaft were converted into a sundial in the eighteenth century. This has a copper dial made by Joseph Park, of Liverpool, which is inscribed: 'John Ellis / James Heyes / Churchwardens / 1761 / Joseph Park fecit.'

The Lychgate

The newest cross is that of the War Memorial which is situated at the north-east corner of the churchyard at the junction of Church Road and the Wiend. The design is by Charles E. Deacon and Sons, of Liverpool, and the work was excecuted by David McGivering of the Wirral Monumental Works in Rock Ferry (with carving by Earp, Hobbs and Miller, of Manchester). It was unveiled on 14 October 1923 by Alderman John Barber, Chairman of the Urban District Council, and was dedicated by Henry Luke Paget, Lord Bishop of Chester. The stone is from the Stancliffe Quarry in Derbyshire. The memorial is sixteen feet high with a canopy. It has an intricately carved shaft and a Latin cross with the sacred monogram [IHS] and the cross of St Andrew. The octagonal base bears the dates of both World Wars and stands on a plinth under which are three steps. The pavement is made of York stone and the surrounding wall uses local stone from the Storeton quarry. The inscription on the plinth (which was modified after the Second World War) is: 'To the glory of God and in grateful memory of the men from this parish who laid down their lives for their King and Country in the Great wars'. The quotation below is from a hymn by Sir John Arkwright (1874-1954):

'O valiant Hearts who to your Glory came
Through dust & conflict & through battle flame
Tranquil you lie your knightly virtue proved
Your memory hallowed in the land you loved'

A roll of honour in the church which is contemporary with the memorial records the names of the men who died in the First World War.

The Parish accounts contain numerous references to the improvements and repairs made to the churchyard. The 'small gate' was repaired in 1788, a 'new gate' was made in 1792; flagstones were purchased for a road through the churchyard in 1797; another new gate was added in 1804, and the 'lower Gateway' was given new steps in 1810. The unprecedented growth in the population was reflected in the need for additional land. In 1835 the unoccupied parts of the churchyard were levelled. Then in 1847 Thomas Green, the Lord of the Manor, provided a plot on the south side for an extension (and burials took place by special licence before it was consecrated). He gave the remaining 2,427 square yards of his land in June 1860. But even this proved inadequate. In 1867 a large plot of land between Rock Lane and Townfield Lane was acquired for use as the Bebington Cemetery. The foundation stone for the Mortuary Chapel in the centre was laid in 1867 and the building was consecrated on 16 June 1868. The cemetery was managed by the 'Burial Board' of St Andrews.

The land to the east of the church was purchased by local trustees in 1919 for future burials and to prevent encroachment of housing upon the church. It was consecrated on 26 October 1940 by Douglas Crick, Bishop of Chester, and continues in use.

The churchyard was redesigned and renovated in May 1968 by K.C. White and Partners of Queen Anne Street, London, and many of the old graves were removed. A full record of the monuments is kept at the Rectory and at the County Record Office in Chester.

Of those that remain, a few deserve mention. By the north-eastern end of the chancel wall there is a square pillar carved with the words: 'Labor/ Vincit / Omnia' / In Memory of Thomas Francis of this Parish who departed this life on the XIV day of April MDCCCL in the LXXXVI year of his age'. He built the gallery at the west end of the church in 1829, made new roofs, helped with the restoration of 1847, and was a benefactor, but he is best remembered as a great eccentric. It is said that he dug his own grave and kept coffins at home in which he and his wife spent their birthdays. He used his skill as a joiner to embellish his modest house at the end of Heath Road and gave it a tower with wooden battlements on which he placed a statue of Britannia and a row of wooden cannon. In the courtyard below he had a wooden dog and several carved figures, including one of himself. All that now remains are his inscriptions on the wall near the entrance to Mayer Park. One says: AR / UBB / I / NGS / TONEF / ORAS / SE /S ['a rubbing stone for asses']; another is a puzzle 'Subtract 45 from 45 That 45 May Remain' [which is 987654321 subtracted from 123456789, which equals 864197532, and adds up to 45]; and a third gives 'thirty shillings' as a clue to the name of the local inn and its owner [Mark (13/4d) Noble (6/8d) of the Two Crowns (10/-)]. The grave is shared with his wife, Ann.

Another important grave is that of Joseph Mayer in the north-west section of the churchyard. It is inscribed: 'Joseph Mayer / Born at Newcastle under Lyme 1803 / Died at Bebington, 1886, aged 82 years/ He strove to enrich in History, Letters and Art / The Town of his birth/ The City where he lived / The Village where he died. / also: Jane Mayer, sister of Joseph Mayer, died August 9th 1892, aged 95.' It commemorates the man who transformed Bebington, giving it a public library and art gallery, and its first public park.

Other graves worthy of note include those of the Lancelyn Green family by the edge of the path leading from the south porch; the grave of William Watson, a High Sheriff of Chester and a benefactor of the church, and the numerous graves of members of the Aspinall family. Several interesting graves are to be found at the east end (near that of Thomas Francis). One by the south buttress is inscribed: 'Little Loo

Loo,/ Died at St Kilda, / Near Melbourne, / Victoria, / December 20th 1853'. And there are also the graves of the Bather family, the damaged base of a cross in memory of Harmood Walcot Banner, the graves of the Victorian Rectors, and a small much eroded stone in memory of Charles Corlett, 'One of Nelson's Heros'.

Nathaniel Hawthorne during his visit in 1853 was struck by the recent date of many of the graves which he said looked older than they were due to erosion. The earliest he saw were 'two standing close together, and raised on low rude arches, the dates on which were 1684 and 1686'. This was because many of the early burials were within the church and those without were for the poorer residents who used wooden crosses. Philip Sulley in *The Hundred of Wirral* (1889) transcribed several epitaphs, including one for a baby who died when only two weeks old: 'Strictly upright in his path through life, he was loved, revered, and most deeply deplored; he has gone a short time before us and rests in Abraham's bosom.' And two for a wife and father:

A virtuous wife, a parent dear,
A tender mother lieth here.
Who is dead as you may see
Prepare yourself to follow me.

Here lies a father we did love,
Departed from us like a dove.
A father we did much adore,
Is gone, but can come back no more.

A Hearse House was built in the eighteenth century when Bebington Parish Church acquired a horse drawn hearse. The earliest reference occurs in the Parish Accounts for 1777 when repairs were needed, and it is mentioned again in 1782 when the wheels were given new rings and spokes. Parishioners were charged 3/- and those from outside the parish were charged 5/-. An additional charge was levied in 1788 when it was ordered 'that every Parishioner shall pay One Shilling and every person not a Parishioner Two Shillings to the Sexton for Cleaning the herse every time they shall use it'. A 'Hearse Book' for 1788-9 has survived and gives details of its use beyond the boundaries of the Parish. The first entries for 1788 are typical: 'March 27th, Going to Walazey and back to Bidston with E. Newby, 10s.6d'; 'April 18th, Going to Moreton and back to Woodchurch with J. Dawson, 9s.0d.' The hearse was equipped with black feathers and plumes (which cost £2.7.6d in July 1792) and remained in use until the middle of the nineteenth century when local undertakers acquired hearses of their own. The Hearse House was rebuilt in 1839 and was afterwards used as a storeroom by the gravediggers and gardeners. It continued to house the trestles and biers used for funerals, including a wheeled bier given in 1911 by Herbert Lancelyn Green (which remained in use until the 1960s).

THE CHURCH CHARITIES

A record of the bequests to the church was kept in the first Parish Register (1625-1661), and at the end of the eighteenth century the names and details of the gifts were copied onto the Benefactors' Board which hangs by the staircase leading to the upper room of the tower. A second board was made in the mid-nineteenth century.

THE COW CHARITY

Among the oldest charities existing in the Cheshire churches are those of the parish cows which were hired out to needy parishioners. At Woodchurch the charity dates back to 1525 when James Goodacre gave 20 marks to 'buye 20 Yoke of Bullocks, which were afterwards, by order of the Commissioners of Pious Uses, converted into Cows, and given to the poor of the said parish'. The Bebington Cow Charity was started in 1620 (or possibly before) and the names of the chief benefactors are recorded on the board in the church. They were William Hulme, of Poulton, who died in May 1620, Christopher Smallshaw, of Bebington, who died in November 1625, and John Briscoe, of Poulton, who died in March 1671. William Hulme left 'three cows to be disposed of by the minister and churchwardens to ye poorest and godlyest parishioners at eight groats *[two shillings]* a year and this hire to be employed for ye increase of parish cows'; Christopher Smallshaw bequeathed a further three cows, and in 1661 John Briscoe gave 'two pounds ten shillings for ye buying of a parish cow'.

The horns of the cows were branded with the initial letter of the parish and those of the Rector, and the animals were grazed on the verges of the roads or on the Common land in Bebington and Poulton. The number of cows and the rules relating to their hire were described by the Reverend Roger Jacson in a letter of 24 November 1815 to George Ormerod:

> 'In 1692,' he said, 'there were 29 cows; in 1712, 26; in 1732, 26; in 1752, 22; in 1772, 16; in 1792, 13; in 1815, 9 cows only; but the number has often been as high as 32. The hire paid for each cow in 1692, and thence to 1755, was 2s. 8d; from 1792 to 1797, 3s; from that date 5s. The rules are, that the cows shall be lent to such persons as the Rector and churchwardens approve, each such person finding a surety, in some substantial parishioner, for the good usage and forthcoming of the cow, on the demand of the Rector and church-wardens, and paying yearly the sum fixed as the hire, and bringing his cow for inspection to the Rectory, now on the 25th April in each year. It appears that the price of a cow in 1692 was something less than £3,

in 1815 it is £9 and upwards. Every encouragement is given to persons willing to advance any portion of the cost of a cow when necessary to buy one; nor are such persons wanting who will give the price of the calf when fat, *viz.* £3 or £4. It should seem that the cows were formerly lent to such persons as held small farms; but such farms having become less in number, the cows are now mostly found with poor labourers and widows; and perhaps a reason may be found in this alteration for the diminution in the number of cows.'

The first register of the cow charity was mislaid before 1815, but the register from 1692 survives and continues to 1861. It lists the 'Principalls' in one column and their 'Suretys' in another, and gives details of the purchase and sale of the animals with other incidental remarks. In 1697 one finds: 'Ye Samuel Briscoe hath turn'd up his cow honestly, & shall have a cow when he has occasion for one. Widow Loon hath turned up her cow unworthily.' In 1708: '1 Cow Bought - £2.07.00; Sold 1 hide a cow it dyed that Josiah Mather had for 2/6d'. In 1711: 'Pd for a marking iron to marke ye parish Cows, 1/-.' An entry for 1748 reads: 'Received the hire of 27 cows, there is 28, but William Lightfoot's cow is not well.' In 1755: 'It was Agreed by the Rector and Church Wardens that Wm Scarisbrick's cow is to be taken from him - by reason he sold a parish cow without consent.' And in 1799: 'Richard Hughes has a parish cow and having nothing to give her, is resolved to turn her up to the parish, and Thomas Hilton is willing to take her and hath 1 ton of hay and promises to do well to the cow.'

The rules governing the inspection of the cows are also contained in the register. 1 May 1744: 'It was then Agreed by the Rector of Bebington and the Church Wardens that for the time to come those parishioners that has parish cows must come and bring in their cow or cows at or before 12 o'clock on ye 1st May yearly or else their cow or cows to be taken from them.' It was changed to the 21st of April in 1778.

The number of cows continued to decline after 1815 (with eight in 1835; six in 1845; four in 1855, and only three in 1860), but the charity remained active until the 1880s. The rents from the hire, the proceeds from the sale of the cows (and of skins and carcasses), and a few small fines from the petty sessions were invested and used for the benefit of widows and sick people in the Parish of Bebington.

THE BREAD DOLE

The bread dole was started by Thomas Gleave, a citizen of London, who in April 1641 gave fifty pounds to the church at Bebington 'to be laid out in Land which remains a stock for the poor for ever, the rent of which being 56s is every Lord's Day laid out in bread, and distributed amongst the poor, as the Minister and Churchwardens see occasion'. Thomas Gleave or 'Cleave' was a man of considerable means, a haberdasher and Alderman of London, who died in 1645. He left similar sums to Woodchurch, West Kirby, Wallasey, Bidston, and Heswall. It seems that he was the father of William Gleave, another Alderman of the City of London, who in 1665 left £500 to found a school at Woodchurch, and they are thought to have been related to the Hockenhulls of Prenton Hall.

The bread board

The carved bread board (now fixed to the west wall) bears witness to the generosity of Thomas Gleave. His name is also found on the lid from the old poor box which hangs alongside, and among the list of benefactors: 'Thomas Gleave citizen of London gave fifty pounds ye encrease thereof to be distributed in bread to the poor every sunday in in ye parish church. Ao. 1641'. The money provided a shilling a week for 'twelve penny loaves of white bread for twelve poor people' and there were extra loaves on holidays.

The original endowment was increased in 1693 by John Eccles, of Tranmere, who 'gave forty pounds ye use thereof to be distributed in bread every Sunday to ye poor of ye parish but especially to those of Tranmore', and John Smith of Storeton who 'gave ten pounds to be disposed of by ye chief Lord and ye Rector for ye good of ye Parish: Ano 1667'. Fines were also used to augment the fund, as on 9 April 1798 when it was decreed 'that if any persons in future shall be seen by the Church Wardens, Clerk, or any Parishioner to throw or sling stones or jump in the Churchyard on the Sabbath Day -such person upon information and conviction before a JP, shall forfeit two shillings and sixpence for each misdemeanour to be laid out in bread for the Poor'. In 1837 the original endowment brought in a rent of £2.16 per annum and the later bequests provided interest of £2.10 on money lent as a mortgage on the Chester and Woodside Turnpike Road. Bread was then being given to all five townships on alternate Sundays.

THE POOR

The money from the bread dole was afterwards invested with other money left to the poor of Bebington. William Glover, of Lower Bebington (whose brass grave plaque survives in the church) 'gave ye use of twenty shillings to ye poor thereof: Ano. 1692'. Richard Carter of Brimstage 'gave twenty pounds to ye parish of Bebington ye interest thereof to be distributed by ye church-wardens and ye overseers of ye poor for every Township: Ano.1698'. The Lords of the Manor were also benefactors: 'Edward Green of Poulton Esqr. gave ten pounds to ye poor of Bebington ye interest thereof to be disposed of by ye chief Lord: Ano 1694' (a bequest made in his will of 20 December 1694, *viz*: 'To the poore of Bebington ten pound for a stock to be disposed on by the master of Poulton'). John Green left the same amount after his death in 1711, as did Thomas Green (though the bequest is not listed).

Two of the Parish bequests relate to specific townships. 'Richard Yockson of Tranmere in ye Parish of Bebington Left to ye Poor of Tranmore one Hundred Pound ye interest to be Distributed Amongst ye Poor of ye Town Every Easter Day for Ever: Ano. 1728'. His will of 23 September 1728 (in which he is named as 'Richard Yorkson, of Great Neston, mariner') stipulated that interest of 5% per annum should be paid to and distributed by the incumbent minister of Tranmere amongst the deserving poor: 'I give devise and bequeath unto the Churchwardens of the Parish of Bebington the sum of one hundred pounds to be paid to them within six months next after my death and to be by them placed out at interest and the interest thereof to be yearly distributed to and amongst the poor belonging to the Township of Tranmore within the said Parish of Bebington in the said County of Chester upon every Easter Monday.'

Thomas Robinson's Charity ('The Allotment' or 'Poor Fields' Trust) was for the poor of Higher Bebington. It was established by an Indenture of 25 November 1746. Thomas Robinson sold two cottages and a plot of land to Thoams Oxton upon trust that the Rector and Churchwardens of St Andrew's would receive the rent and use it to assist the poor of Higher Bebington. Further land was added and by a Deed of Exchange dated 17 February 1842 the 'Poor Fields' were transferred to the King family. They afterwards built Christ Church in Higher Bebington, and in 1896 claimed the right to adminster the Charity on behalf of the poor of the new parish. The land was sold to Sir William Lever in September 1915.

Several benefactors are not listed on the boards. Henry Hockenhull of Liverpool, Gentleman, who died on 22 March 1682 gave £5 to the 'Poore of the Parish of Bebington '; William Porter left £2.10, and there were gifts of £10 from Mrs Heasley, and £20 from Clarke Aspinall. The most notable omission is Clayton Conroy, a ropemaker of Birkenhead, who died on 24 March 1860 and left £1,000 for the poor of Bebington. The 'Conroy Trust' drew its income from properties in Stanley Terrace, New Ferry, and afterwards from shops in the New Chester Road (numbers 78-96) and was constituted by deed of conveyance in 1873. The qualifications for relief (in the form of bi-monthly payments) were based on residence in the township of Lower Bebington. It continues as a functioning trust with as many as forty beneficiaries.

The second board (on the south wall by the tower) gives details of three Victorian benefactors. 'John Fitchett Esq., Late of New Ferry in this Parish, gave Fifty Pounds in the year 1839 the interest therof to be distributed in Bread to the Poor attending the Parish Church.' Notice of the bequest was given to the Rector in February 1839 when Joshua Wagstaff of Winnington explained that though Mr Fitchett had died intestate (on 20 October 1838), he had left instructions for this sum of money to be given to Bebington Church and his sister and heir was anxious to carry out his wishes. The other bequests mentioned on the board were secured upon box pews and these ceased to earn income when letting was discontinued in 1871. On Easter Day 1847, 'Mr Thomas Francis, of Lower Bebington, Gentleman, gave the sum of One Hundred Pounds secured upon seats numbered 83-84-85 and 86, the interest to be distributed in Bread to the Poor attending the Parish Church'. And 'Mr Richard Jones, of Lower Bebington, Gentleman, who died 19th April 1859, gave by his Will to the Rector and Churchwardens of the Parish Church the Pew No.23 therein, and also £20 (less legacy due. £2) the rent of the Pew and interest of the money to be applied by them to Bread for the Poor of the District.'

THE PARISH SCHOOL

The deed founding a school at Bebington is dated ll February 1655, the parties being Richard Greene, Lord of the Manor, Sir William Stanley of Hooton, and others, and it states that a plot of land 'to wit, Ten acres in the Lees which already is measured and set out by Agreement for the maintenance of a School, shall be and remain to and for the same use for ever'. The Lees were near the modern Port Sunlight Station and within a year the acreage had been doubled by enclosing other common land. The benefactions board in the church records the gift: 'Inhabitants of Bebington at ye enclosing of a Common gave twenty acres of land towards ye maintenance of a schoolmaster eligible by chief lord and ye Rector. Ano. 1656.'

The school was first located in the Belfry as Bishop Gastrell discovered when he visited Bebington in about 1718. 'Here is a Free school,' he said, 'the Master of which receives £5.6.0 per annum, the Rent of twenty acres of land given by ye inhabitants upon enclosing of a Common. No School House, but the Master teaches in ye Belfry.' The master at that time was the Parish Clerk, Thomas Crompton, who died in 1719 (the brass tablet from his grave can be seen at the east end of the south aisle). There was then a gap of six years until his son was appointed in his place. The delay was caused by uncertainty over who had the right of nomination. According to a Memorandum sent to the Bishop of Chester, the former Lord of the Manor had claimed the sole right, while the late Rector had 'always declared' that he shared the right of nomination. They now agreed to act together as Governors. When putting forward Thomas Crompton the younger, 'the first time as there ever was a presentation of a School-Master of Nether Bebington' offered to the Bishop, they said:

> We whose names are hereunto subscribed as being left Trustees to Edward Green Esq. haveing the right of presenting to the School of Bebington now vacant do present unto your Lordship Thomas Crompton son of the late School-Master of the said School, Humbly praying that your Lordship would grant him a Licence to the said School with the right and appurtenances, as Witness our hand this 24th day of August 1725.
>
> Thomas Green/Priscilla Green/Hugh Poole

The school was still in the Belfry in 1778 according to the Episcopal Visitation Returns, and Thomas Crompton remained as schoolmaster even though he was in his late seventies and was thought 'no longer capable of that close attendance which is necessary'. After his death on

11 January 1791, the school moved to the Vestry at the east end of the church. This building, which rested on the corbels below the main window, is shown in a drawing of 1809 by T.R.Rickman. It had a sloping roof with two exterior doors and a plain three light window, and there was access from the church through the door on the right of the communion table. It was in use when Ormerod was compiling his *History of Cheshire* (1818). 'A room attached to the end of the church,' he said, 'which is a considerable injury to the elegant appearance of the fabric, is used as the school.' Certain names, initials, and dates presumably of the pupils can still be seen (with later graffiti) on the east walls, and the grooves which resemble ancient runes or arrow marks are said to have been made when sharpening slate pencils.

The old Vestry was demolished in 1827 and for a time the school was held in the south aisle of the church. Then in 1828 Sir Thomas Massey Stanley gave the land in Acre Lane or 'School Lane' on which two (still extant) schoolrooms and a house for the schoolmaster were built by voluntary subscription. It seems that another building was used while they were being constructed as the Parish Accounts for 1835 include the 'cartage of stone and timber from the Old School to the New Built School'. The description given in the Report of the Charity Commissioners in 1837 also refers to the old school. They found it in bad condition and blamed the great age of the schoolmaster who was between seventy and eighty years old and had held the position for nearly fifty years. He had charge over 140 pupils (one of whom was Edward Sothern, the actor) who paid 2d a week towards his salary of £40 per annum.

In March 1856, Major Orred, of Tranmere Hall conveyed 3,060 square yards of land in Green Lane to the Rector and Churchwardens for a new school. A 'neat and spacious structure in the Gothic style' was built the following year at a cost of £500 (raised by voluntary subscription). The 'Bebington National School' had three teachers and could accommodate 150 boys, 100 girls, and 100 infants. It was extended in 1888 and 1901, and was refurbished in 1923.

The St Andrew's Church of England Primary School as it is now known moved to new premises in Townfield Lane in 1974. These were destroyed in an arson attack on 24 January 1992. The school continued in temporary accommodation at the Teachers' Centre in Acre Lane, Bromborough, until new buildings were erected on the Townfield Lane site, to which the school returned in 1993.

The interest of £20 per annum from the 'School Lands' went towards the salary of the schoolmaster in the eighteenth and nineteenth century, but the value of the land increased many times when the 'Sunlight Soap' factory moved to the adjoining fields in the late 1880s. In 1888 William

Owen, who was acting on behalf of the Lever Brothers, offered the Rector £150 per acre, and after consultation it was decided to sell the land and invest the proceeds. The 'Lower Bebington School Lands Foundation' became a Trust in 1924 with the Lord of the Manor and the Rector as trustees. It provides 'Educational Exhibition, Maintenance Allowances, and other Grants' to children and young persons resident in Bebington.

ST ANDREW'S PARISH HALL

The Parish Hall is built on land alongside the Rectory and is of recent date. The fund was launched on 26 August 1954 at a meeting of the Parochial Church Council. A service of commendation was held on the site on 2 February 1959, and the foundation stone was laid by the Rector's wife on 4 April 1959. It was designed by a firm of local architects, Patterson and Macauley, and built by Richard Costain, Ltd. It has an asymmetrical pitched roof which covers a large hall and six smaller meeting rooms on two levels. The main hall has a stage at one end and a kitchen and vestibule at the other. There are two staircases leading to the upper floor and gallery. The walls are faced in brick; the floors are of 'Granwood', the gallery balustrade of mahogany, and the external woodwork of red cedar. The wrought iron balustrades for the staircases, the internal gallery, and the balcony over the main entrance, incorporate St Andrew's crosses and are by Quiggin Brothers. The building was dedicated by the Lord Bishop of Chester, the Right Reverend Gerald Alexander Ellison, on 19 September 1959.

The hall is used for the Sunday School, Bible Classes, Church Lads' Brigade, Girl Guide Companies and Brownie Pack, the Young Churchmen's Fellowship, Women's Fellowships, prayer meetings, the Missionary and Men's Fellowship, and other organisations of the Church Fellowship.

THE CHURCH LADS' BRIGADE (BEBINGTON COMPANY)

The Church Lads' Brigade was founded in 1891 by Walter Mallock Gee and the St Andrew's Bebington Company No.219 was enrolled on 24 October 1893 with Captain W. Williams as the first Commanding Officer. Bernard Ormerod took over in 1895 and was in charge until his death in 1927. The band was formed in 1898, and a Drill Hall was built in Bromborough Road in 1912. During the First World War members of the Brigade formed the two Battalions of the Kings Royal Rifle Corps.

Bernard Ormerod provided the capital for the Drill Hall and left the building to the Church on his death. It was demolished in the 1950s and the proceeds from the sale of the land went towards the new Parish Hall. 'Ormerod Court' stands on the site and there are gardens nearby with gates in his memory.

Major S.C.Frodsham took over the command of the Bebington Company in 1927, J. Bernard Hughes in 1938, Major Leslie Hughes in 1940, Major Edgar Jones in 1956, Captain Robert Wood in 1968, and Captain Thomas Lindsay in 1971. The Church Lads' Brigade and the Church Girls' Brigade were amalgamated at national level in 1978, but the St Andrew's Company remains a Boys' Brigade and is divided into three sections: the Young Boys Corps for those aged seven to eleven; the Junior Training Corps for those between ten and thirteen, and the Senior Corps for boys aged thirteen to twenty-one. The Brigade aims to extend Christ's Kingdom among young people and lead them to a personal relationship with Jesus Christ, and the activities include parades and drill, camps, reviews, Bible classes, football matches, and shooting practice.

CHURCH MISSIONARY ACTIVITY

Since the middle of the last century St Andrew's has had a proud record of missionary activity both at home and abroad. Missions across the world, in Africa and China looked to Bebington, and the tradition continues to this day with great efforts being directed towards South America. Colin Bazley, who was brought up in Bebington and has had close links with the South American Missionary Society for over thirty years, was appointed Bishop of Chile in 1969 and is now also Presiding Bishop for the whole of Southern South America.

THE STORETON MISSION

The Storeton Mission was founded by Canon Feilden and a licence 'for the Performance of Divine Service in Storeton School Room in the Parish of Bebington' was granted on 23 November 1867. The Storeton estate was owned by Sir Thomas Brocklebank, but was subsequently sold to W.H. Lever who, after the school was declared redundant in 1913, converted it into the Storeton Working Men's Club. In 1912 W.H.T.N. Rainey had transferred the services to cottages in Storeton following a disagreement with the owner of the property and Mrs Brocklebank, but under H.E. Boultbee, the old arrangement was re-established and the Church had the use of the Club for Divine Service on Sundays and during one day a week.

After the First World War the Leverhulme Estate Office drew up plans for the development of Storeton, and at the end of 1928 three acres of land were set aside for the provision of a church. A decision was taken to build a Parochial Hall with a capacity of between 200 and 250 people for use during the first stage of the development, as this could then serve as the Church Hall if a larger Church were built. The Storeton Mission Building Fund was planned at the end of 1929 and began seeking contributions in April of the following year. The Leverhulme Estate offered the land at a ground rent of 2/6 per annum until the completion of the building, after which a rent would be charged or the church could exercise an option to purchase the freehold.

The plain brick building with stone cappings was designed by Major Duncan Campbell, F.R.I.B.A., and the foundation stone was laid in February 1936 by Lady Bates, the wife of Sir Percy Bates, chairman of the Cunard White Star Line. The building cost a little over two thousand pounds, of which three-quarters had been raised by the time of its completion in October 1936. The Leverhulme Estate waived the rent for the first year and in January 1938 the Church with the assistance of Diocesan Board of Finance purchased the freehold. All outstanding loans and debts were paid off by December 1940.

The new mission church was named St Philip's and was dedicated by Dr G.F. Fisher, the Bishop of Chester, on 4 October 1936. The church bell was the gift of Sir Percy Bates and came originally from the Mauretania; the sanctuary chairs were constructed from the old roof timbers of St Andrew's, Bebington, and other gifts included chancel rails, a pulpit and reading desk, a lectern, an electric clock, a hymn board, and an organ.

The planned redevelopment and expansion of Storeton village never took place, partly because of the changed circumstances within the Leverhulme Estate and partly because of the war and the post-war planning restrictions. Regular services continued to be held by curates and lay readers, but by the late 1970s the size of the congregation had fallen to such a low level that the Parochial Church Council decided to suspend services from October 1977. Thereafter the building was used for a Tuesday Women's Fellowship and for an occasional funeral. A working party of the Parochial Church Council (J.E. Parry, C.H.B. Watson, Mrs L.C. Williams, and N.D.W. Thomas) was established in 1979 to review the future of the church building. As it had been dedicated and not consecrated, it was possible to sell the building for non-ecclesiastical use, and on 13 October 1980, after close consultation with the residents of Storeton village, the decision to do so was taken by the Parochial Church Council. Four years later, on 4 November 1984, the building and part of the land passed into the ownership of R.T.Porter who converted the hall into a private residence known as Claremond. The proceeds of the sale were used to create the St Philip's Fund, and part was used to buy a second curacy house in Acreville Road, Bebington.

A small parcel of land to the rear of the building is retained by the Church and let to a grazing tenant. This is to preserve an interest in Storeton against the day when the redevelopment of the village might again require a church to minister to the needs of the community.

THE RECTORS OF BEBINGTON

According to the *Domesday Book* there was a priest at 'Pontone' in 1087, and a deed from the reign of Henry III in the Rylands's Library in Manchester (No.1592) refers to 'Henrico, persona de Bebington'. Until the dissolution of the monasteries, the Rectors were presented by or on behalf of the Abbot and Convent of St Werburgh in Chester. The names of the Rectors, the date of their institution, their patrons, and the cause of the vacancy as listed in the Lichfield and Chester Registers, are as follows:

1272-86: SIR RALPH DE MONTALT, son of Robert de Montalt (who held lands in the Manor of Bebington) and brother of Sir Roger de Montalt (Constable of Chester, 1232-60); Rector of Neston from 1258; Rector of West Kirby, from 1264; and Rector of Bebington (held in plurality) from 1272. Died 1286.

1286-1316: PHILIP GERARD (named in the Plea Rolls of Edward I [23-24] as 'William Gerard'), serving as Rector in 1294 and presumed to be the immediate successor of Ralph de Montalt.

1316-31: ROBERT DE NOTTINGHAM, instituted June 1316. Died 1331.

1331-38: WALTER DE NORTON (named in a charter of 1335 [British Library, Add. MS. 36998] acquitting him of tithes in Astbury, Chester), instituted 1331. Died 1338.

1338-42: THOMAS DE CAPENHURST, clerk (presbyter), the son of Madoc de Capenhurst (Sheriff of Chester, 1327); parson of St Mary-on-the-Hill, Chester from 1335; instituted as Rector of Bebington in September 1338 under the patronage of John of Arden. He resigned in 1342 when appointed Rector of Monte Alto in the Diocese of Assaf under the patronage of Queen Isabella.

1342-46: JOHN DE HALE, instituted as Rector in July 1342. Resigned 1348.

1348-49: JOHN MAUNT [DEMANUTE/MANUT], Dean of the Free Chapel of St Burian in Cornwall until 1348 when 'the Deanery was seized into the King's hands, by reason that Mr John de Manute, then incumbent, was a Frenchman'. He was permitted to exchange the Deanery with John de Hale and was instituted as Rector of Bebington in July 1348. He exchanged the living the following year for that of Skelyngham.

1349-55: PETER DARRAN who held the living at Skelyngham until he exchanged it with John Maunt; instituted as Rector of Bebington in September 1349.

1355-81: JOHN DE WETEFELD [WETTEFELD/WETFELD], instituted as Rector of Bebington in November 1355 (Lichfield Register), and named in the Plea Rolls of Edward III [29] and the Recognition Rolls of 1367; also Rector of Swettenham and Hanley. Said by Ormerod to have been instituted in 1356. Died 1381.

1381: WALTER DE BEBINGTON, appointed in error. An inquest presided over by the Archdeacon of Chester declared that his presentation as Rector in 1381 by the Abbot and Convent of St Werburgh was void, 'the five years demise being unexpired at the date of the death of the last Rector, Wetefeld'.

1381-1400: [HUGH DE FFARYNTON]/ROGER DE FFARYNTON [FARYNGTOUNE]. 'Sir Hugh de ffarynton' was instituted as Rector on 28 April 1381 under the patronage of John of Davenport and was referred to as 'of good fame' in the inquest which deposed Walter de Bebington. His name is also found in a bond with Sir William Stanley, dated 25 September 1382. Ordained 1378; Rector of S. Peter-le-Bailey, Oxford, 1378; Rector of Radwinter, Essex, 1378; treasurer of Salisbury, 1386; Rector of Burton-by-Lincoln, 1392. Roger de ffaryngton is named as the Rector of St Andrew's, Bebington in an appeal to the Bishop of Lichfield of 8 August 1393 (Harleian MS 2179) and in another of 3 February 1398 (Ryland's Library, No.1748). There is no reference to any vacancy caused by the resignation of Sir Hugh, but it is likely that he made over the living in 1386. Roger de ffarynton died 1400.

1400-22: WILLIAM WARMYNCHAM [DE WEMYNCHEM/DE WERMYNGHAM], instituted as Rector of Bebington on 2 May 1400. Ordained priest, 25 February 1401. He was granted a licence to study at Oxford for two years on 8 December 1401, and was given leave of absence from his benefice for periods of up to one year on 1 October 1404, 29 December 1404, and 24 October 1406. Died April 1422.

1422-64: ROBERT DEL BOTHE [bothes/BOOTH], possibly the son of John Bothe and brother of William and Laurence Bothe who both served as Archbishop of York, instituted as Rector of Bebington in April 1422. In 1423 he was one of the sureties for John of Kingsley, and in 1429 he entered into recognizances to Richard of Bolde. He is named in a mandate of 24 September 1448 from William, Bishop of Coventry (Ryland's Library, No.1365). Died 1464.

1464-1507: JOHN CARLELE, instituted as Rector of Bebington on 8 June 1464 under the patronage of Thomas Stanley and his wife, Eleanor, and Richard Carlele. Died 1507.

1507-11: NICHOLAS CHAUNTERELL [CHAUNTRELL], the son of Richard and Margaret Chaunterell, instituted as Rector of Bebington in October 1507. The Lichfield and Chester registers disagree on his subsequent appointments. John Brereton is said by one to have been appointed in 1511 on the death of Robert [*sic*] Chaunterell, while the other states that Randle [Ralph] Lawton was appointed in 1528 following the resignation of Nicholas Chaunterell. Ormerod [1882] says: 'It is possible that a Robert Chauntrell succeeded Nicholas, and another Nicholas succeeded Brereton. The last mentioned Nicholas is stated to have resigned on a pension of £23.6.8 which Lawton upon oath promised to pay him for the term of his natural life. On Lawton's death, the Bishop confirmed this pension to Sir Nicholas, out of the fruits and emoluments of the living.' The other possibilities are that John Brereton assumed the Rectorship at Bebington between 1511 and 1528 while overseeing the rebuilding of the church and returned it to Nicholas Chaunterell after his departure, or he may have succeeded Robert to a post other than that of Rector. The Chaunterells owned land in Lower Bebington through the marriage of William Chauntrell to Alice, daughter of Thomas de Bold, Constable of Chester Castle (who died in 1464), and they were instrumental in the rebuilding of the east end of Bebington Church. The 'biggest window on the south side' of the church bore the Chaunterell coat of arms, raised in 1523 in memory of the Rector's parents (Harleian MS.2151).

1511-28: JOHN BRERETON, the third son of Sir Randle Brereton of Shocklach, brother of Sir William Brereton (beheaded, 17 May 1536, on account of his association with Anne Boleyn); said by one register to have been instituted as Rector of Bebington on 14 March 1511, resigned in 1528. Rector of Hatford, Berkshire, from 1509; Dean of Astley, Warwickshire, from 1509; Canon of St Paul's, London, and Prebendary of Hoxton, from 1631; Rector of Christleton Church, Cheshire, 1532-7; Rector of both moieteies at Malpas, Cheshire, from 1532 (the only Rector who ever held both livings); master of St Bartholomew's Hospital, from 1532. Pardoned, 9 March 1532, for obtaining papal dispensation for holding benefices in plurality; Rector of St Mary-on-the-Hill, Chester, from 1534; Rector of Longstanton Church, Cambridgeshire, from 1534; Dispensed on 10 January 1535 to hold a fourth benefice; Vicar of Buckland, Berkshire, from 1535; Rector of Compton Bassett, Wiltshire from 1535; Rector of Astbury, 1535-42; Canon of St Asaph and Prebendary of Venall. Master Mason for Cheshire and Flint, 1537-42; a friend of Thomas Cromwell, whose daughter lived at Neston. He died 1542 and his name appears on his parent's tomb at Malpas. He was responsible for the rebuilding of the east end of Bebington Church and for the church at Astbury.

1528-31: RANDLE [RALPH] LAWTON, instituted as Rector of Bebington, 22 April 1528 on 'the resignation of Nicholas Chaunterell' [*sic*]. Died 1531. His Will (in modernised spelling) was as follows:

In the name &c. The 17th day of May 1531. I Rauff Lawton clerke parson of the parish church of Bebington sick &c. and my body to Christian supulture. I will that my funeral expenses be made and done in competent and convenient manner according to my degree at the disposition of my executor. To the three orders of Friars at Chester to be evenly distributed among their three houses 4 shillings for to have their prayers for the wealth of my soul and all Christian souls. To the Convent of the monks of Saint Werburgh in Chester to have dirige and masses of requiem by them said and celebrated in their monastery ten shillings. To my mother Mawde Massy six pounds, thirteen shillings and four pence. To Sir John Hareson curate of Bebington above said ten shillings, he to sing and say a trental for my soul and all Christian souls. To the same Sir John my sarsanet typett and my best black hose; to John Whyksted my chamelet jacket and my best doublet of black chamlett and a shirt and my boots; to Sir William Johnson priest my riding gown and my cloth typet lined with sarsanet; to Margret Mydylton daughter to Robert Mydylton fletcher, late of Chester deceased toward her marriage forty shillings. Unto Roger Sclater, Hugh Sclater and Randle Sclater to every one of them a pair of hose and a pair of shoes. And to Nicholas Brygge my old worsted jacket in recompense of their pain and labour had and one about me in my sickness. To Henry Vernon my grey horse called Gryme and a pair of riding shoes. The residue of all my goods after my debts paid and my funeral expenses deducted I will to be at the disposition of my executor for the health and wealth of my soul. I order &c. Mr John Lawton clerke parson of Astbury my executor. These being witness: Sir William Johnson of Chester, chaplain, John Whyksted and Henry Vernon with other Yeven and made the day and year above said.

Among the debts owing by the testator are the following "To my master Sir John Lawton parson of Astbury of him by me borrowed at diverse times in my necessities fifteen pounds, ten shillings. For the pension of Bebington to be paid at the Feast of Saint James next coming twenty-two pounds, six shillings and eight pence. To the Vicar of Bromborouh by the assignment of the Abbot and Convent of Chester for the pension of Bebington due at midsummer next thirteen shillings and fourpence."

1531-35 DAVID POLE, instituted as Rector of Bebington, 23 August 1531. Graduate of All Souls' College, Oxford; Vicar of St Giles, Oxford,

1528-31; Rector of Cheriton, Devon, 1530; Canon of Lichfield and Prebendary of Tachbrook; Archdeacon of Salop; Canon and 5th Prebendary of St John's, Chester; Rector of Longford, Derby; Rector of East Dereham, Norfolk; Archdeacon of Derby; Rector of Wadenhoe, Northants; Bishop of Peterborough, 1557. On the accession of Elizabeth I signed a letter with two other bishops begging her to return to the Catholic faith; deprived of his bishopric on refusal to sign oath of supremacy, but allowed to live freely in retirement. Died 1568.

1535-43: RICHARD GWENT: instituted as Rector of Bebington in [or before] 1535. Fellow of All Souls' College, Oxford, 1515-28, law dean, 1524-5; BCL[common law], 1518; BCnL [Canon law],1519; DCnL, 1523; DCL, 1525; principal of the Canon law school, 1525, of the civil law school, 1528; Vicar of St Giles, Oxford, 1523-4; Rector of Tangmere, Sussex, 1528; Rector of Leckhampton, Gloucestershire, 1529-31; St Leonard's Foster Lane, London, 1530-4; Rector of Doynton, Gloucester, before 1534; Canon of Lichfield and Prebendary of Pipa Parva, 1531; Prebendary of Longdon in Lichfield, 1531-43; Rector of Newchurch, Kent, 1533-43; Rector of St Peter's, West Cheap, London, 1734-43; Canon of Lincoln and Prebendary of Leighton Ecclesia, 1534-43; Rector of North Wingfield, Derbyshire, 1534-43; Archdeacon of London, 1534-43; Canon of St David's and Prebendary of Llandewi-Aberath, 1535-41; Canon of Llandaff and Prebendary of Caerau, 1535-43; Rector of Walton on the Hill, Lancashire, 1536-43; Archdeacon of Brecon, 1539-43; Rector of Bredon, Worcestershire, 1540-3; Prebendary of Llangan in St Davids, by 1541; Archdeacon of Huntingdon College, 1542-3; Canon of St Paul's, London, and Prebendary of Totenhall, 1543. College of Advocates, London, 1526; Kekeper of the spiritualities of Coventry and Lichfield; official principal of court of Canterbury in 1533; Prolocutor of the Convocation of Canterbury, 1536-43; Dean of Arches, 1541-3; Counsel for Queen Catherine (of Aragon) at the divorce proceedings, 1529; Chaplain to the King by 1532; visited Merton College, Oxford, September 1535 as Archbishop Cranmer's commissary. Died 1543; Will dated 21 July 1543, proved 6 February 1544.

1543-54: JOHN HARRISON [HARRYSON], instituted as Rector, 25 August 1543, under the patronage of Richard Hyde. John Harrison was the father of Margareta Harrison, his heir (and wife of Richard Holmes of Tranmere) who was buried at Bebington on 20 September 1589. After the dissolution of St Werburgh's Abbey the advowson of Bebington Church was acquired by Sir Richard Cotton who on the death of Richard Gwent used the right to instal the former parish clerk as Rector. The Dean and Chapter of Chester Cathedral acquired a licence from Edward VI on

14 May 1553 (Rylands Library, No.1626) to alienate Sir Richard Cotton (in exchange for an annual rent of £603.18s.10d) from the manors and tenements of the former Abbey, and from the advowson and donations of the churches of Christleton, Bebington and Astbury which had formerly belonged to the abbey.

1554-6: THOMAS RUNCORN [RONCORNE], instituted as Rector of Bebington, 9 May 1554; graduate of Oxford University: BA, 1518; MA, 1521; Archdeacon of Bangor, 1529; Rector of Offord, Cluny, Huntingdonshire, 1534; licensed by the King to hold not more than four benefices with cure, 4 November 1535; Rector, East Woodhay, Hampshire, 1536; Vicar of Bowden, Cheshire, 1536; Canon and Prebendary of Winchester, 1541-54; Provost of St Elizabeth College, Winchester, 1541; Rector of Crawley, Hampshire, 1541; Rector of Llanrhaiadr, Debighshire, 1543; Vicar of Waverham, Cheshire, 1554; Canon of Lincoln and Prebendary of Sanctae Crucis, 1555; also advowson of Leckasforde, Hampshire; died [October] 1556; Will, 21 September 1556, proved 2 July 1557: 'My body to be buried in the chancel of Bebyngton Church, in case of death in that parish ... To Roger Saston [Sefton], clerk, my advowson of Bebyngton ... £20 on the poor in Bebyngton parish (one third to the church) ... To the church of Bebyngton a vestment, superaltar and corporas.'

1556-70: ROGER SEFTON, instituted as Rector of Bebington, 10 October 1556, under the patronage of John Grice. He took the Oath of Supremacy in 1563. Buried at Bebington, 26 December 1570.

1571-2 THOMAS BENNET. On 1 February 1571 the advowson of the church of Bebington was sold by Thomas Green, of Farnehill, Cheshire, to Sir Rowland Stanley, of Hooton (Ryland's Library, 1455); on 6 April 1571 Sir Rowland Stanley petitioned Edmund, Archbishop of York to admit Thomas Bennet, clerk, to be Rector of Bebington in place of the late Roger Sefton (Ryland's Library, No.1456).

1573-81: LUKE [LUCAS] GILPIN: instituted as Rector of Bebington in 1573, resigned May 1581; born, Kentmoor, Westmoreland; Graduate of Trinity College, Cambridge, scholar, 1560; BA, 1561-2; MA, 1565; BD, 1576; Fellow, 1562; Proctor, 1574-5; ordained priest (London), 3 April 1569; Vicar of Chesterton, Cambridgeshire, 1572; Archdeacon of Derby, 1577-87; Prebendary of Southwell, 1581-7. For Bebington he paid first fruits on 9 February 1573, and resigned in 1581 when appointed to Southwell. Died October 1587. Gilpin's appointment was the cause of dissension between Sir Rowland Stanley who had proposed Edmund Meyrick, and Grindal, the archbishop of York who favoured Gilpin. Sir Rowland brought an action against the archbishop in the Palatine Court at Chester to vindicate his right of patronage, but the decision rested with the Ordinary, and as this was Grindal himself and his authority superseded that of the Bishop of Chester, he failed to have the decision overturned. A grant of the tithes of Storeton to Sir Rowland Stanley by Luke Gilpin, dated 6 August 1575, is to be found in the Ryland's Library (No.1588).

1581-1602: JOHN NUTTER, instituted as Rector of Bebington 1581; graduate of Brasenose College, Oxford, 1566; BD; Dean of Chester, 1589-1602. Died 1602 (his successor as Dean was not appointed until 1603, and Ormerod therefore assumed he had died in 1603).

1602-47: HUGH POOLE, second son of Ralph Poole, of Whitby, gradson of Sir William Poole, of Poole; married Amicia (who died April 1624); graduate of Peterhouse, Cambridge: admitted, pensioner, 30 March 1594; BA, 1596-7; MA, 1600; Fellow, 1599-1605. Presented to the living of Bebington by the patron, John Egerton, of Egerton, and instituted on 4 June 1602. In May 1647 he was deprived of the living and the Rev. Josias Clarke was appointed by the Committee for the Relief of Plundered Ministers. Died, 6 June 1647; buried at Bebington, 9 June 1647.

1647-62: RALPH POOLE, son of Hugh Poole (above); baptised at Bebington on 20 October 1616; married Amicia Dobson, of Liverpool, at Bebington, 24 August 1648; graduate of Emmanuel College, Cambridge: admitted, pensioner, 24 May 1632; BA, 1653-6; MA, 1639. Despite sequestration in May 1647 of his father's living at Bebington, he was 'by divers of the said parish, by force thrust into the said church', and appears from the registers to have continued to enjoy it until his death on 5 April 1662 to the entire discomfiture of the Rev. Josias Clarke. He was buried in the church on 9 April 1647 and is commemorated on the small brass tablet (to the right of the altar): 'Radulphus Poole Hugoni patri tam suggesto quam sepulchro eodem successor collectus fuit ad patres Aprilis 5, 1662.'

1662-88: RICHARD STONES, of Lancashire; second husband of Amicia Dobson, of Liverpool, former wife of Ralph Poole (above), and father of John Stones, the Cheshire Antiquary (1680-1735); graduate of St Catherine's College, Cambridge: matriculated, as sizar, Easter 1655; BA, 1658-9; MA, 1662. Died, 10 October 1688, buried at Bebington, 12 October 1688.

1688-1708: HUGH POOLE [2], son of Ralph Poole (above); baptised, Bebington, 18 September 1649; school, Wrexham (Mr Lewis); graduate of St John's College, Cambridge: admitted, pensioner, 4 May 1667; BA, 1670-1; MA, 1674; Incorp. at Oxford, 1681; ordained deacon (Chichester), 5 May 1673; priest, 21 December 1673. Presented to the living of

Bebington in 1688 by David Bavand. Died 1708.

1708-16: JOHN HALL, son of Thomas Hall, of Eccles, Lancashire; graduate of Brasenose College, Oxford, matriculated, 10 February 1698-9; BA, 1702. Died 1716.

1716-39: HUGH POOLE [3], son of Hugh Poole (2), baptised at Bebington, 26 August 1691'; school, Prescot, Lancashire (Mr Waring); graduate of St John's College, Cambridge; matriculated, 1708; BA, 1711-12; MA, 1715; ordinaed deacon (London), 12 June 1715; presented to the living at Bebington by John Slater, and instituted on 7 July 1716. Died 1739.

1739-53: JAMES ADAMS, MA, Vicar of Estham, former curate at Bebington, presented to the living by the patron, Roger Jacson, on 5 May 1739 and instituted, 12 May 1739. Resigned in favour of Simon Jacson, 17 August 1753, but remained in the service of the church at Bebington.

1753-77: SIMON JACSON, nephew of Hugh Poole [3], son of Simon Jacson, merchant of Chester (who married Mary Poole, 1721); born, Chester, 2 April 1728; married, Anne Fitz-Herbert, of Derby, 20 November 1749, by whom he had eight children, among them Frances, a novelist (died 1842), and Maria, author of *The Florist's Manual* (died 1829); school, Bury, Lancashire (Mr Lister); graduate of St John's College, Cambridge, admitted, pensioner, 30 June 1744; BA, 1748-9; MA, 1761; ordained deacon (Lichfield), 24 September 1752; priest, 17 June 1753; patron of the living at Bebington where he was instituted on 20 August 1753; resigned in favour of his son, 15 July 1777 and moved to Stockport; Rector of Tarporley, 1787-1808; died 15 April 1808.

1777-1826: ROGER JACSON, eldest surviving son of Simon Jacson (above); born, Bebington, 9 July 1753, baptised 25 July 1753; twice married: [1]. 19 March 1777, to Frances Gibson, of Romaldkirk, Durham, [2] 27 May 1801, Mary Anton Johnson, of Wallasey. Graduate of St John's College, Cambridge: admitted, pensioner, 1 February 1770; Scholar, 1773, BA (13th wrangler) 1774; Foundress Fellow, 4 April 1775-7; ordained deacon (Ely), 2 June 1776; priest (Sodor and Man), 27 July 1777, Presented to the living at Bebington by his father, 15 November 1777; J.P. for Cheshire, and for forty years Chairman of the Court of Quarter Sessions in Chester (which post he filled 'with honour to himself, and benefit to the county' - Ormerod). Died 6 March 1826, buried at Bebington. Memorial tablet on the east wall of the Chancel and a hatchment on the north wall. The graves of the Rector, his son, Shallcross Jacson (who died 21 August 1853), and grandson, Roger Jacson (died 23 September 1853) are on the site of the old vestry: 'Beloved, revered, and most deeply lamented. Practical religion was the guide of his eminently useful life: He taught her precepts pure and undefiled, and in himself exemplified how cheering and how social are her paths.' There is a tablet at the west end of the north wall, for his son,John Jacson, who died on 6 March 1799 (aged 20), after a 'painful illness of seven years continuance'.

1826-62: ROBERT MOSLEY FEILDEN, the son of Robert Feilden, of Didsbury Hall, Cheshire, Ancoates, and Rolleston Hall, Staffordshire; born 4 July 1794; married, 18 February 1822, Frances Mary Ramsay; graduate of Brasenose College, Oxford: matriculated, 18 October 1813; barrister-at-law, Lincoln's Inn, 1818; graduate also of Magdalene College, Cambridge: BA, 1823, MA, 1824; ordained deacon, 1825; priest (Lichfield and Coventry), 1826; instituted as Rector of Bebington, 5 August 1826, presented by John Feilden; senior magistrate of the Hundred of Wirral; died, 14 May 1862; buried at Bebington. The graves of the Rector and of his wife (who died 1 October 1893), are on the site of the old vestry - next to those of his sisters, Frances Mary Feilden (1826-56) and Eliza Ann Feilden (1822-1915). A reredos and a stained glass window were erected in memory of the Rector by the parishioners, fellow magistrates, and friends, but only the brass plaque survives, as the reredos was replaced and the window destroyed in the Blitz.

1862-1907: GEORGE RAMSAY FEILDEN, second son of Robert Mosley Feilden (above); born 8 July 1828; married, 24 August 1865, Margaret Priscilla Feilden (third daughter of Joseph Feilden, of Witton Park); educated at Eton; graduate of Christ Church, Oxford: BA, 1850; MA, 1853; ordained deacon, 1853; priest (Oxford), 1854; curate of Stratfield-Mortimer, Berkshire, 1853-6; Stone, Worcester, 1856-9; and curate of Bebington, 1859-62; Rector of Bebington from 1862; Honorary Canon of Chester, 1873-88; Canon Residentiary from 1888; Rural Dean of Wirral, 1885-97; Proctor in Convocation for the Cathedral Chapter, 1890-5. Died, 13 October 1907; buried at Bebington, 16 October 1907. The graves of the Rector and of his wife, Margaret (who died 14 June 1885), are on the site of the old vestry. The screens across the north and south aisles and the furnishing of the south chapel serve as a memorial to Canon Feilden and were 'erected by his family, parishioners & friends'.

1907-13: WILLIAM HENRY THOMAS NORMAN RAINEY; married, 4 May 1909, Miss Nicholson; episcopal Scholar, Manchester, 1895; Pembroke College, Oxford 1902; assistant curate of St James', Heywood, Lancashire, and curate-in-charge, Heap Bridge, 1897-1902; assistant curate, South Hinksey, Oxfordshire, 1902-5; Vicar of Clanfield, Oxfordshire, 1905-7; appointed as Rector of Bebington in November 1907; instituted by the Bishop of Chester in a private ceremony, 11 January 1908, and inducted the same day by Archdeacon Barber (in a hastily arranged service). Resigned September 1913. Vicar of St Paul's, Hampstead, 1913-20; Rector of Knebworth from 1920; publications, *The Church Impotent here in Earth* 1918. Died 1924.

1913-18: GEORGE ADAM FORD; educated, Royal Institution School, Liverpool; graduate of Trinity College, Dublin, MA, 1899; Fellow of Allahabad University 1904; ordained deacon, 1882; priest (Lincoln), 1883, curate, Plumtree, 1882-3; Nettleham, Lincolnshire, 1883-4; St Peter-in-Eastgate with St Margaret, Lincoln, 1884-5; Diocesan Inspector of Schools for Lincolnshire, 1885-8; Vicar, Cherry-Willingham, 1885-8; Chaplain, Bengal Ecclesiastical Establishment, Fort William, Calcutta, 1888; served in Mandalay, Upper Burma, Field Force (Imperial Order of the Crown of India, medal and clasp), 1888-90; Chaplain, Ranikhet, 1890-1; Lucknow, 1891-2, 1894-7; Mhow, 1892-4; [furlough 1897-81; Muttra, 1898-9; senior chaplain, All Saints' Cathedral, Allahabad, 1899-1905; editor of the *Lucknow Diocesan Chronicle*, 1900-5; Archdeacon of Lucknow, Chaplain of Naini Tal, and Examining Chaplain to the Bishop of Lucknow, 1905-8; Commissary of Lucknow, 1908-28; Vicar, Honingham with East Tuddenham, 1908; St Paul, South Hampstead, 1908-13; instituted as Rector of Bebington, 21 November 1913; resigned 1918. Rector of Ashill, Norfolk, from 1918; Rural Dean of Breccles, 1922-9. Died 31 January 1930. The statue of St Andrew in the niche to the left of the altar and a plaque on the wall close by were given in memory of the Rector's eldest son, Kenneth George Haslam Ford, O.M., a Lieutenant and Machine Gun Officer in the Cheshire Regiment who fell in France on St Andrew's Day, 1915, and was buried at Bailleull.

1918-41: HUGH EDMUND BOULTBEE, son of the Reverend James Boultbee, Rector of Wrangthorne, near Leeds; married, 1894, Amy Lumb, of Doncaster; educated, Leeds School (Dr Henderon), to 1886; served apprenticeship as an engineer with Hudswell, Clarke, & Co., Leeds; graduate of Durham University (President of the St Cuthbert Society): L.Th & BA, 1891; MA,1897; ordained deacon, 1892; priest (York), 1893; curate, St James's, Doncaster, and curate-in-charge of the daughter church at Hexthorpe, 1892-7; St Paul, Southwark, 1897-1901; Vicar, St Peter's, Clifton (Bristol), 1901-5; Grey Friars, Reading, 1905-15; Christ Church, Surbiton, 1915-18; instituted and inducted as Rector of Bebington, 1918; Rural Dean of North Wirral, 1941; died 26 November 1941; buried at Bebington, 29 November 1941 (the funeral service conducted by his son, the Reverend James Boultbee, Vicar of St Mark's, New Ferry). The graves of the Rector, his wife, Amy (who died 2 August 1940) and their daughter, Margaret Joyce Boultbee (who died 10 February 1989) are on the west side of the churchyard. The reredos behind the altar was erected in his memory in 1954, and his notes on the church were published in 1955, *The Parish Church of Bebington.*

1942-54: ARTHUR GORE BERNARD: younger brother of William Bernard, of Birkenhead; born in Liverpool, 1874; worked in business for fourteen years; graduate of St Catherine's College, Oxford: BA, 1903, MA, 1908; Wycliffe Hall, Oxford, 1904; ordained deacon, 1904; priest (Liverpool), 1905; curate, St Anathasius, Kirkdale, 1904-9; curate-in-charge, St Nathaniel's Mission, Fazakerley, 1909-18 (where he oversaw the building of the Church of St Nathaniel); Vicar, Emmanuel, Everton, 1918-42; Chaplain of West Derby University, 1918-42; Canon Diocesan of Liverpool, 1934-42; Canon Emeritus from 1942; Proctor in Convocation, 1935-42; member of the Church Assembly and of the Archbishop of Canterbury's Church and State Conference; co-founder of the Liverpool Evangelical Tutorial School (for young businessmen entering the Ministry); appointed Rector of Bebington, January 1942; instituted by Dr Douglas H. Crick, Bishop of Chester, and inducted by the Very Reverend R.V.H. Burne, Archdeacon of Chester, 28 March 1942; died, 20 March 1954; funeral at Bebington, 23 March 1954 (Memorial Service, 28 March 1954). The graves of the Rector and of his wife, Kathleen (who died 11 December 1959) are on the west side of the churchyard near that of his immediate predecessor.

1954-67: ANTHONY GREVILLE POUNCY: born 1914; graduate of Queen's College, Cambridge: BA, 1937; MA, 1941; Tyndale Hall, Bristol, 1937; ordained deacon, 1938; priest, 1939 (Sarum); curate, St John's, Weymouth, 1939-41; Vicar, Christ Church, Coventry, 1941-6; editor/secretary of the Bible Church Missionary Society, with permission to officiate in the Diocese of Rochester, 1946-54; instituted as Rector of Bebington by Dr Douglas H. Crick, Bishop of Chester, and inducted by the Very Reverend R.V.H. Burne, Archdeacon of Chester, 22 June 1954; resigned 1967; Vicar, St Peter's, Woking, 1967-79; retired; permission to officiate at Portsmouth, 1981. Died 4 August 1993.

1967-79: WILLIAM MICHAEL DERMOT PERSSON; born 1927; graduate of Oriel College, Oxford; BA, 1951, MA, 1955; Wycliffe Hall, Oxford, 1951; ordained deacon, 1953 (Dover, for Canterbury); priest, 1954 (Canterbury); Canon, 1982; curate of Emmanuel, South Croydon, 1953-5; St John's, Tunbridge Wells, 1955-81; Vicar, Christ Church, Mymms, Barnet, 1958-67; Rector of Bebington 1967-79; member of the General Synod for the Diocese of Chester, from 1975; Commissary, Chile, from 1977; Vicar, St John's, Knutsford and Toft. 1979-82;

Examining Chaplain to Bishop of London, 1981; Suffragan Bishop of Doncaster, 1982-1992.

1979-93: GEOFFREY MARTIN TURNER: born 1934; educated at Sandhurst; Oak Hill Theological College, 1960; ordained deacon, 1963; priest, 1964 (Rochester); curate, St Stephen's, Tonbridge, 1963-6; Heatherlands, Dorset, 1969-73; Vicar, St Peter, Derby, 1969-73; Christ Church, Chadderton (Greater Manchester), 1973-9; Rector of Bebington 1979-1993 Honorary Canon of Chester Cathedral from 1989. Rural Dean of Wirral North 1989, Member of the General Synod for the Diocese of Chester. Appointed Archdeacon of Chester 1993.

1993 - STEPHEN LYNN JAMES: born 1953 graduate of Middlesex Polytechnic B.A; Oak Hill Theological College; ordained deacon 1986; priest 1987 (Norwich) curate Holy Trinity Heigham 1986-89: Assistant Rector St. John's Shaughnessy Vancouver 1989-93; Rector of Bebington 1993-

THE NEW CHURCHES

The Parish of Bebington originally comprised the townships of Higher and Lower Bebington, Poulton-cum-Spital, Storeton, and Tranmere (including the modern townships of Rock Ferry and New Ferry), and for a time the Rector of Bebington had the right of appointing the curates to Overchurch.

UPTON, OVERCHURCH [Parish of Overchurch], the advowson passed from the Dean and Chapter and Chester to the Stanleys of Hooton, thence to the Jacsons and Feildens who appointed curates from Bebington (Rev Edward Newton, 1813; Peter Wilson, 1823; C. Sanderson, 1828; W. Cleminson, 1829); sold to William Webster, 1831, thence to William Inman, of Upton Manor, who in 1868 paid for the new church of St Mary; architect, John Cunningham.

ST CATHERINE'S, TRANMERE [separate Parish of Tranmere St Catherine, 1842], from Tranmere Township; foundation stone laid 1 January 1831; consecrated 15 October 1831; re-built 1875-6 by J. Francis Doyle, re-consecrated 1 June 1876; new tower and spire added in 1879.

ST PETER-ON-THE-ROCK, ROCK FERRY [separate Parish of Rock Ferry, 1844], from part of Higher Bebington Township; chapel, 1838; land and money for new church given by R.W. Barton; architects, Hurst and Moffat; foundation stone laid by the Rector of Bebington 16

April 1841; first service 8 September 1842; consecrated 4 June 1844. Bomb damage, 1941.

ST PAUL'S, TRANMERE [separate Parish of Tranmere St Paul, 1858], from part of the township and new Parish of Tranmere; land given by George Orred, with donation of money by his brother, John Orred; architects, W. & J. Hay; foundation stone laid 23 May 1854; opened 25 November 1855; consecreated 10 October 1857.

CHRIST CHURCH, HIGHER BEBINGTON [separate Parish of Higher Bebington, 1877], from part of the new Parish of Rock Ferry; land and stone given by Rev. Joshua King and George King; architect, Walter Scott; foundation stone laid by Mrs William Willis 1 August 1857; consecrated 24 December 1859; steeple added in 1885.

ST LUKE'S, LOWER TRANMERE [separate Parish of Lower Tranmere, 1883], from parts of the new Parishes of Tranmere St Catherine and Tranmere St Paul; architect, G.E. Grayson; consecrated 18 October 1881.

ST MARK'S, NEW FERRY [separate Parish of New Ferry, 1888], from part of Lower Bebington township; built 1865-6; architect, Edward Haycock.

HOLY TRINITY, POULTON [separate Parish of Poulton-Lancelyn, 1987], from the Parish of Bebington, land and house (Poulton Hey) given by Roger Lancelyn Green; first conveyance 13 March 1972; dedicated 12 September 1977; foundation stone of new church laid by Roger Lancelyn Green 1 February 1987; architect Paterson Macaulay and Owen, dedication of the new church of the Holy Trinity by the Rt Rev. William Persson (former Rector of Bebington) 12 September 1987; consecration of the Sanctuary and Side Chapel by the Rt Rev. Ronald Brown, Bishop of Birkenhead, 26 July 1992.

PARISH RECORDS

The Parish Records are preserved in the Cheshire County Record Office, deposited December 1968, July 1969, May 1983, July 1984, May 1986, and they include: Early Registers, 1558-1812; Register of Christenings, 1813-1935; Register of Marriages, 1754-1930, Register of Banns, 1785-1824; Register of Burials, 1813-1909; documents relating to the Church Buildings and Churchyard (including Faculties, Plans, and Citations), 1829-1925; catalogue of graves, 1968; Churchwardens' Accounts and Vestry Minutes, 1774-1926; Charities (including the Cow Charity Register and the Conroy Trust papers, 1692-1966; Schools, 1854-1974: Bebington Burial Board, 1916-24; and other miscellaneous papers. The County Record Office also houses the Diocesan records relating to Bebington church and the appointment of the Rectors.

The Parish Registers of Bebington, Co. Chester, from A.D. 1558 to 1701, Edited and Annotated by Francis Sanders, M.A. (Oxon) and Wm. Fergusson Irvine, Liverpool: Henry Young and Sons, 1897; cr.8vo, viii, 242pp, red cloth; printed in an edition of one hundred copies only.

THE PARISH MAGAZINE:

Started January 1864 (incorporating the national *Parish Magazine* until December 1895, and the *Parish Monthly*, 1896-8; changed to a larger format in January 1911; afterwards renamed *The Lychgate,* and now published as a Parish newsletter, *Bebington Life.*

GUIDE BOOKS

COX, EDWARD W.: *Architectural History of Bebington Church.* A Paper read before the Historic Society of Lancashire and Cheshire, 4th November 1897. By Edward W. Cox. Liverpool: Printed by Thomas Brakell Limited, 1898; grey paper covers, 26pp. An offprint of the article cited below.

PEARCE, J.P.: *The Church of Saint Andrew, Bebington, Cheshire.* Descriptive Notes by Joseph Pearce, F.R. Hist. S., with a foreword by the rector, Hugh E. Boultbee; Liverpool: Service Guild (The Service Guild Series of Guides), n.d. [ca.1925], 39pp (with text on rectos, advts. on versos), illus. from photographs (4), wrappers, [3d.].

BOULTBEE, H.E.: *St. Andrew, The Parish Church of Bebington, Wirral, Cheshire,* A Short History and Guide written by the Late Rev. H.E. Boultbee, M.A., Rector (1918-1941) with subsequent revision, sketches from original pen and ink drawings by Mrs A.E. Macleod [and a preface by A.G. Pouncy]; Gloucester: British Publishing Company Ltd, n.d. [June 1955], 15pp, wrappers.

GREEN, ROGER LANCELYN: *St Andrew, The Parish Church of Bebington*, by Roger Lancelyn Green, with a foreword by the Rector, W.M.D. Persson, with 4pp of illustrations from photographs; [Liverpool: Liverpool Letter Press], n.d. [December 1968], 23pp, wrappers.

SELECT BIBLIOGRAPHY

HOLME, R., *Cheshire Monuments [III]*, Harleian MS 2151, containing details of the stained glass windows in Bebington Church, 1629.

RICKMAN, T., 'Drawings of Churches', 1802-1812, BM [Add,37,803] (contains two drawings of St Andrew's, made in 1809 and 1811 (the first shows the vestry at the east end).

ORMEROD, GEORGE, *The History of the County Palatine and City of Chester,* London: 1818; second (revised and updated) edition, 1882.

'SAXON' (pseud. of the Rev. William Elstob), 'Architecture' (Bebington Church), *Gentleman's Magazine*, August 1844, New Series, Vol.22 [pp.186-7] (on the state of the church and the need for restoration).

MORTIMER, WILLIAM WILLIAMS, *The History of the Hundred of Wirral*, London, Whitaker and Co, 1847 [pp180-92].

REED, CHARLES, 'Bebbington Church [sic]', *Proceedings of the Liverpool Architectural and Archaeological Society*, Vol.1 (Sessions 1848-9, 1849-50), Liverpool, 1852 [pp.5-12]. The paper was read on 11 October 1848.

HAWTHORNE, NATHANIEL, *Passages from the English Note-Books of Nathaniel Hawthorne*, Boston: Houghton, Mifflin & Co./ London: Strahan & Co. 1870, 2 vols (includes descriptions of his several visits to Bebington Church).

SULLEY, PHILIP, *The Hundred of Wirral,* 1889, Birkenhead: B. Haram & Co. [pp.301-15].

COX, EDWARD W., 'The Architectural History of Bebington Church,' *Transactions of the Historic Society of Lancashire and Cheshire,* Vol.49 (New Series, 13), Liverpool, 1898 [pp97-122].

BUDDEN, CHARLES, W.: *Rambles Round the Old Churches of Wirral,* Liverpool: Edward Howell, Ltd., 1922.

[ANON], 'St Andrew's Hall, An architectural description of the construction of the new building', *Builder*, 1 January 1960 [pp6-8], ills. plan.

CLARK, PETER E., 'The Organ at Bebington Parish Church,' *Organ*, October 1963, Vol.43 [pp94-1011].

In addition to the works cited above, several invaluable articles and edited texts are to be found in the *Cheshire Sheaf* [1898-1921], the transactions of the several Cheshire and Lancashire Historical Societies, and the publications of the Chetham Society.

ACKNOWLEDGEMENTS

The author wishes to acknowledge his debt to the earlier histories of the church and to the authorities quoted in the list of sources; also the librarians and staff of the libraries consulted, in particular those of the Cheshire County Record Office and the Bebington Public Library. Special thanks are also due to the former Rector, Geoffrey Turner, who offered advice and encouragement during the composition of this work, and to others within the parish who contributed information and advice, among whom particular mention must be made of Nicholas Thomas, Norman Higgins Jean Hindley and Geoffrey Stone.